THE SILVER BULLET

C000038755

This book provides practical guidance for corporate decision makers, project managers, project engineers, and for those wishing to grasp the key issues that define project success. The book represents a distillation of years of practical experience and offers a clear and concise 'blueprint' for how to approach projects and their management.

This book is designed to be 'clean and simple' in its delivery – allowing the reader to immediately have 'take-aways' that could be implemented within a project, adding value to any approach dealing with the key common problems and issues that arise within the project medium. The book can be applied to a wide range of scenarios in which project management is required – from setting up an organisation, creating distribution networks, bringing new technology to market, and to designing a leadership and training architecture within an organisation.

The book, in addition to being a go-to reference book on project management for professional project managers and business leaders, is also ideal for postgraduate and undergraduate students studying project management. It is written to be user friendly yet provides a wealth of information and tips that will enhance the reader's knowledge and understanding of managing projects.

Christopher Lennon is Director of Stone Falcon Corporate and Legal Consulting Ltd. The company works internationally within the domain of project management from both a training and consulting perspective – specialising in helping projects in trouble and strategic aspects pre-initiation.

"In this book, Chris Lennon pragmatically articulates and navigates the dichotomies that regularly exist between the creative and norm challenging academic teachings and the experience developed over time which 'grounds' the project manager through years of practice. His ability to help the reader make sense of the key issues and the use of a 'silver bullet' to cut straight to the point makes this a realistic, supportive read within a field that is traditionally, perhaps by internal design, seen as complicated and fraught with financial, reputational and operational dangers."

Steve Johnson, *MSc, FCIPS Chartered Ex Dip, FCILT, Head of Commercial Management, TEXO*

"Whereas a lot of books on project management, espouses much theory and philosophical concepts, Christopher's book is far from that. It is a truly pragmatic approach, which incorporates many lessons learnt at the 'coal face' of leading projects. His distinction between Critical Success Factors (CSF's) and Key Performance Indicators (KPI's) is of particular value to the project management practitioner. These two concepts are often confused as being the same thing, whereas they are in fact distinctly different and serves different purposes. Likewise, the role of the project sponsor is very clearly delineated. A great read if you are serious about project success!"

Nic Loubser, *Business Strategist, Managing Partner, PROFECTUS*

"Chris Lennon has, over many years, consistently been a very popular teacher of Project Management on our Undergraduate and Postgraduate programmes. His teaching style is greatly appreciated for his engaging and captivating – indeed absorbing – approach, which has always delivered the Learning Outcomes in a manner which has had a big impact on the students. I am delighted to see he is putting this track record to good use in a significant new book, which I am sure will be both as useful and as popular as his teaching has always been."

Dr Paul Davidson, *School of Engineering, Aberdeen University*

"A no-nonsense review of fundamental approaches to keep projects on track, from concept to delivery. When the heat blurs the horizon, many project managers will find help here for keeping control."

Alex Chwetzoff, *Oilfield multi-disciplinary projects manager*

THE SILVER BULLETS OF PROJECT MANAGEMENT

Christopher Lennon

Routledge
Taylor & Francis Group

LONDON AND NEW YORK

First published 2022
by Routledge
2 Park Square, Milton Park, Abingdon, Oxon OX14 4RN

and by Routledge
605 Third Avenue, New York, NY 10158

Routledge is an imprint of the Taylor & Francis Group, an informa business

British Library Cataloguing-in-Publication Data
A catalogue record for this book is available from the British Library

Library of Congress Cataloging-in-Publication Data
Names: Lennon, Christopher, 1967– author.
Title: The silver bullets of project management / Christopher Lennon.
Description: Abingdon, Oxon ; New York, NY : Routledge, 2022. | Includes index.
Identifiers: LCCN 2021011367 (print) | LCCN 2021011368 (ebook) | ISBN
    9781032037813 (hbk) | ISBN 9781032037820 (pbk) | ISBN 9781003188964 (ebk)
Subjects: LCSH: Project management. | Management.
Classification: LCC HD69.P75 L463 2022 (print) | LCC HD69.P75 (ebook) |
    DDC 658.4/04—dc23
LC record available at https://lccn.loc.gov/2021011367
LC ebook record available at https://lccn.loc.gov/2021011368

ISBN: 978-1-032-03781-3 (hbk)
ISBN: 978-1-032-03782-0 (pbk)
ISBN: 978-1-003-18896-4 (ebk)

DOI: 10.4324/9781003188964

Typeset in Bembo
by Apex CoVantage, LLC

CONTENTS

INTRODUCTION

BEGINNING

The field (science, discipline, art) of project management continues to grow in importance to the corporate world. Organisations are increasingly aware that the 'project methodology' approach to achieving strategic objectives makes a lot of sense. Traditionally, there was often a 'disconnect' between the corporate and operational levels of an organisation – the corporate level perhaps having unrealistic expectations of what was achievable as to what the operational capability of the organisation actually was. This, in the author's experience, is often a major cause for concern, as it can become a primary driver for the manifestation of conflict, stress and tension.

Project management itself is at best a bit of an elusive beast – we all tend to have our own way of classifying what we consider it to be. While there is nothing inherently wrong with this diverse range of opinions and thinking it can sometimes be a precursor to confusion. Several years ago, while teaching at a local university on their Master's programme, I used to open my lectures with a simple question right at the outset. I would ask the class to voice their opinions as to what they considered project management to be. As one would expect, there was a wide number of examples shouted out, ranging from shipbuilding to dam construction, to highways, etc. My next question would then be whether or not anyone would consider a monthly shopping trip to fall within the ambit of project management. A large majority of students would feel that no, this was not the case. Some of the more 'lateral thinkers' among them (or perhaps

DOI: 10.4324/9781003188964-1

those of a more suspicious nature) would begin to hesitate and look thoughtful.

The truth of the matter is that most of us think of 'projects' and 'project management' as being involved with large and complex issues – the building or creation of something like some of the examples mentioned above. If we consider projects and the management of them from the starting point (i.e. the often referred-to 'iron triangle' of project management) we will see that there are three basic operating criteria that will enable the successful delivery of a project, these being that the project (no matter what it is) is delivered on time, to the correct specification (quality) and within the allotted budget. Simple? Yes, in theory – not so much in reality though.

To return to the example of a monthly shopping trip: it most definitely could be considered a project – all the required elements are there – and you will likely have a budget; there will be transportation and logistical issues, you might well have to outsource specialists (i.e. childcare) and you may have an inescapable time limit in which to deliver the objective (contractual stipulation such as the agreed amount of time for childminding). Further to this you will also see behaviour making 'trade-off' decisions due to budgetary and quality constraints.

The point of this example is simple: we are all project managers every day of our lives –often unaware of this fact. The purpose of this book is to provide some degree of clarity as to what a project is and what project management is about, from the standpoint of adding value and understanding to the reader. This book will be useful to the layman, practitioner or student alike as a quick reference guide and hopefully an enjoyable source of information on the subject. The book is divided into a number of short chapters in an attempt to be both concise and relevant to the topic in question.

Chapter 1 begins with a discussion of the 'project methodology' and its various ramifications for the modern organisation, followed by subsequent chapters covering critically important issues such as the project lifecycle, the management of stakeholders and just what exactly it is that a project manager should be doing with their time. There is also an examination of some of the underlying, less obvious (but still centrally important) intangible aspects such as conflict resolution and the role played by learning and experience.

Following on from these chapters, the book then begins to 'drill down' to examine some of the more specific issues surrounding the successful delivery of projects such as the project business case and the role played by the project sponsor. The 'project scope' is discussed in detail, as is the management of financial acuity (budgetary management and responsibility), Project Interfaces and the implications for project management and the strategic goals and objectives of the organisation as a whole.

The discussion then moves into an examination of the 'mechanics' or 'operational activities' of scheduling a project, the allocation and assignment of resources to where they are needed when they are needed, some of the approaches taken to scheduling and a discussion on the importance of understanding what 'precedential activities' mean to a project. The implications of mutually exclusive and inter-dependency of activities will be assessed in terms of their ramifications for work structuring as per a project schedule utilising concepts and methodologies such as work packages and work breakdown structures.

The final chapters examine issues such as the management of resources, the concept of 'project crashing' and project 'fast tracking' as well as the importance of lead time management – particularly regarding those lead times that are deemed 'critical' and project inventory management issues.

THE PROJECT METHODOLOGY

This book's Introduction alluded to the project methodology and its many ramifications to modern-day organisations with good reason. Increasingly, the rate of change within operating environments continues to accelerate due to technological progression, ever more remote and challenging physical environments, political machinations and social/economic factors. Scarcity of resources and limitations in experience and knowledge – particularly within the aforementioned more 'extreme' operating environments – all point to an increasingly consistent approach to adopting a project methodology in order to achieve corporate objectives.

Where the project methodology comes into its own is from the perspective of structure and control. Many projects are representative of a foray into the unknown for the organisation, often with some serious strategic drivers or initiatives riding on a successful outcome – consider, for instance, a market penetration project that takes the organisation away from its core competencies, potentially high risk and likely to be subject to a high level of uncertainty. What the organisation normally lacks in these types of endeavours is either experience within the target environment, knowledge as to how to 'do things' or, realistically, a combination of both. This in itself underpins the strategic dimension to utilising the project methodology – it is a sensible way to make a limited and controlled expedition into the unknown. If successful, the organisation can capitalise on the experience and knowledge gained. It is also worth pointing out that 'lessons learnt' will also have a certain transferability, i.e. underpinning future endeavours, avoiding previous mistakes, etc. If the project proves to be an utter and complete failure,

DOI: 10.4324/9781003188964-2

then the risk and financial exposure to the organisation as a whole is generally minimised.

The project methodology allows the organisation to clearly define the amount of resources that will be devolved to an initiative in a structured and logical manner; thus the risk factor is at least (in the majority of cases) 'contained' within some known budgetary boundaries.

Many projects, as well as for the reason mentioned above, are also the harbingers or agents of change – again the project methodology allows a greater level of control and structure to be imposed upon a change initiative – perhaps providing an element of 'comfort' to those driving the process. Change is inevitable – my earlier mentioned points regarding the increasing strategic significance of corporate usage of the project methodology are often proven by the fact that there is an upward trend in the adoption of this approach by organisations faced with the implementation of change programmes. Change is scary – it is more than likely that a particular initiative will face opposition of some sort, yet the project methodology can prove to be a powerful tool in demonstrating the structured and controlled approach to be adopted – thus easing some concerns by displeased parties within the organisation. The project methodology will demonstrate control across many areas of potential concern such as cost (a defined budget is allocated); time (the project will run to a clearly defined schedule); and quality (there will be a minimum specification of deliverable).

Coupled to all the points raised above, the project methodology will also clearly identify what the key performance indicators (KPIs) and critical success factors (CSFs) are. KPIs might be the achievement of a particular milestone in a project's execution, or the end of a phase (i.e. the 'stage gate approach'). They might also be represented by financial (budgetary) indicators. CSFs might be a particular level of quality achieved, or some defined time-based goal (e.g. successful critical lead time management).

Further evidence of the linkage with corporate strategy or strategic ambition is evidenced by the extension of the project methodology – many organisations today utilise both 'programmes' of projects and 'portfolios' of projects, both of which may actually be more representative of the execution of core capabilities to achieve longer term outcomes and goals – the major difference between the two being whether or not the projects in question are working towards a common objective/deliverable. There is also a question of scale. A programme of projects may involve a number of parallel projects that could have direct interdependencies, but may not – they will all however be representative of a piece of the overall goal/deliverable/objective. Portfolios can consist of a number of programmes of projects and thus could be thought of as the 'macro' or overarching strategic usage of the project methodology.

This chapter has made a case for the importance and usage of the project methodology in achieving organisation goals and aims – not only from a strategic perspective but also from an operations perspective. But, like anything, there are both advantages and disadvantages to its utilisation. The main advantages are as follows.

First, as mentioned previously, should the project be representative of a 'journey into the unknown' for the organisation, the financial costs and liabilities will be strictly contained within a designated budget, thus limiting exposure and mitigating risk (only a defined amount of resources will be committed to any particular project, so in effect 'damage' will be controlled should things go awry (in the tangible sense of materials, personnel and money). Second, in the intangible sense such as corporate reputation, it is unlikely that the adoption and utilisation of a project methodology would 'contain' any fallout, unless the project was deemed 'top secret' and the project team were sworn to silence and assuming that nothing was to leak out (e.g. if a project's operations were going to cause some kind of environmental pollution or disaster).The author would suggest that any responsible organisation would not want to operate projects in this way, though regrettably there have been many examples of such practices that have only been revealed due to 'whistle blowers.'

From the operational or tactical perspective of actually implementing and successfully delivering a project, another key advantage of the project methodology is that it requires or facilitates the need for detailed planning. While a plan, if properly followed and executed, is a great help, it should never be rigid and inflexible. Often the best way to build robustness in a plan is that it contains some element of flexibility allowing for changes and modifications as either the situation on the ground, the physical environment or customer requirements change. This aside (but always kept in mind), project planning is an art form in itself – the main difficulty is to recognise that the 'Devil really is in the details' yet not to 'over-engineer' the plan to the extent that its complexity, size and detail become unwieldy and of minimum practical use to the project manager having to execute it.

As mentioned above, a project plan must be robust – the need to make changes to it and to have an awareness of the likelihood of this requirement is often helped if the organisation has a system of checks and balances that allow for accurate and meaningful monitoring of project activities as per the defined schedule. The ability to review progress thus far against budgeted and planned progress is truly invaluable to the project practitioner. This is often reflected by the usage of 'milestones' or 'stage gates' that represent a point of achievement at a particular point in time.

The main disadvantages are likely to be relatively 'simple' matters that may result from lack of experience and/or mismanagement. As we have established, the very fact that projects are often a foray into the unknown – a departure from the organisations' core competencies or skills, and that through the utilisation of the project methodology there is an assigned budget – mistakes and cost/time overruns will result in resource consumption that may simply be irreplaceable. A strong advantage of the structure imposed by the project methodology is that it enables focus on essential project performance elements vital to delivery such as KPIs and CSFs – both discussed in later chapters. This will allow a greater degree of control as the project progresses – particularly if it is of a 'change' nature as mentioned above – seeking new revenue streams or competing within new markets.

Table 1.1 summarises the main advantages and disadvantages of the project methodology.

Table 1.1 The project methodology: key advantages and disadvantages

Advantages	Disadvantages
1 'Damage control'	1 Departure from 'core' activities
2 Limitation of risk	2 High risk
3 Planning and control	3 Competition for resources
4 Monitoring and review	4 Multiple constraints
5 Configuration	5 Lack of knowledge and experience
6 Learning and experience	6 Conflicting stakeholder agendas

IDENTIFYING PROJECT RISK AND OPPORTUNITIES

As we have established in Chapter 1, projects will often represent a higher-than-normal risk factor. In some industries such as the 'upstream' exploration and production (E&P) segment of the international oil and gas business, projects can represent an extreme level of risk. It is important to point out at this stage a brief maxim that explains the relationship between risk and reward:

> The further into the future that is being planned for the greater the level of uncertainty. The greater the level of uncertainty the greater the risk. The greater the risk the greater the reward.

Contemporary research suggests that there are three main attitudes towards risk within practically any context: Individuals (and organisations) that are risk takers, those that are risk averse and, by far the largest segment, those who will attempt to balance the level of risk to the level of reward. It is important to understand with crystal clarity that the level of risk that is acceptable not only depends on an attitude or culture but also on the level of perceived reward. This is why in the E&P business mentioned above projects often represent an almost prohibitive level of risk – but if successful the returns can be enormous, more than justifying the cost, expense and time invested.

A key problem facing all organisations is that there is almost always likely to be some form of constraint in resources – they might not be available, or perhaps the organisation lacks significant capital or a 'war chest' to dip into in order to fund project activity; this should be a critical factor when assessing a potential project

DOI: 10.4324/9781003188964-3

opportunity. Often the process of making a decision is based on identified alternatives and options and various component elements that are contained within the maxim above. Formally, the process is often known as 'Project Investment Appraisal' and involves the utilisation of a number of financial parameters in order to aid in the decision-making process. Some of the most common techniques utilised are the 'IRR' (internal rate of return), NPV (net present value) and a 'breakeven analysis.' These techniques are more advanced than the level intended within this book. Suffice to say, IRR is simply a discount rate that is closely linked with NPV. It is a discount rate at which the future cash flows from a project equate to a zero value. The higher the value of the IRR, the more attractive a project will be to an organisation.

When speaking of NPV, this is the future value of money expressed in what it could buy today. Put simply, £1.00 today might only have a true value of £0.90 in five years into the future. Why this is significant is because one of the key factors when making investment choices across multiple potential projects is the 'timing of the returns.' Some of the options might appear to yield smaller amounts, but if they are closer in time, the value of every £1.00 might be higher (i.e. in two years' time £1.00 might have a value of £0.97), thus making the 'real value' of the returns stronger. All projects will be subject to the 'timing of the returns' – which is why these techniques are important. Lastly, the breakeven analysis is exactly what it says it is – simply a calculation that estimates or establishes some future point in time when the project would have made no loss (breakeven) and from that point onward start to make profitable returns. All these factors are inextricably linked, all have a component element of 'time' and all help to inform the investment decision-making process of an organisation that might have several projects upon which it could embark/invest in.

An obvious precursor to the successful delivery of a project is going to be the effective management of risk. Risk takes many forms – from pure 'economic risk' (i.e. financial risk) to 'human risk' (the risk to the health and safety of employees engaged upon a project). As stated above, the quantification of the risk level often determines why it is that the organisation has embarked upon a particular endeavour in anticipation of reaping the potential rewards. Some risks may be considered to be industry specific (i.e. the risk of radiation exposure within the nuclear industry), whereas others might be of a more generic species (i.e. the risk of physical injuries to workers through things such as slips, trips and falls).

Although some might suggest otherwise, the process or methodology of managing risk is relatively simple – use a large dose of common sense. If you are the individual tasked with drawing up the risk management plan (or indeed are the risk 'manager' on the project), your starting point should be to identify all associated risks as far as possible. Some risks may be of a more 'latent' nature and may not be immediately apparent – start with those that are obvious. The next step (working from identified risks) is to attempt to 'rank' them somehow. Generally speaking, risks tend to be ranked according to several (common-sense) criteria. First, what is the likelihood of the risk occurring (some models of risk management utilise the phraseology of 'frequency' here)? Second, if a risk does manifest itself, what are its likely impacts on the project? Having designed the basic architecture of managing the risks, if an identified risk appears to represent a threat to the success of the project, then we need to put into place some form of strategy for dealing with that risk. Broadly speaking, there are a number of strategies for dealing with risk that are common and make sense. First, the organisation could simply avoid the risk by deciding not to proceed with the project, perhaps selecting a better option (or – as is an oft-forgotten option in project investment – simply do nothing). Second, the organisation could share the risk (consider joint ventures (JVs) in the E&P industry). Thus, if a risk was to manifest, the exposure to it is halved (assuming two partners in a JV – there could be more).

Third, the organisation could transfer the risk – perhaps by entering into some form of contractual arrangement with a specialist contractor (e.g. a company that will manage radioactive materials) – and thus the organisation is no longer involved with the management of this risk. Fourth, the organisation could implement factors that will reduce or mitigate both the severity and likelihood of a risk manifesting (e.g. mandatory wearing of personal protective equipment for all employees embarked upon activities that involve an identified risk such as eye protection for operators of spinning/cutting equipment). Lastly, in some cases the organisation will simply decide that it is going to 'own' the risk and manage it. This could be because the organisation itself is actually the specialist provider or has the most specialist knowledge in handling and controlling a risk (perhaps the organisation itself is the most knowledgeable about the handling of radioactive sources – it is therefore the best-placed entity to ensure that associated risks are managed properly).

These three steps or stages should form the backbone of your risk management plan. There are a multitude of tools, techniques and software all geared towards managing risk – some are better than others and some may suit certain environments better than others. This choice will be dependent on case-specific requirements.

From a project perspective, the major 'types' of risks that often lead to cost overruns (and therefore to a negative impact on budgetary limitations) are listed below:

1 Schedule delays
2 Incorrect scope/scope creep
3 Unforeseen/random events

COST OVERRUNS

Any project has a defined set of resources, the financial element being represented by a budget. If cost overruns occur through delays or mismanagement of the budget then this risk is a serious one. Many projects remain incomplete or representative of wasted time, money and effort due to running out of funds – even if more funds are allocated, the increased delivery cost will always have a negative impact on the projects' bottom line (profitability) – potentially to the significant detriment of the parent organisation. Cost overruns can sometimes occur simply due to a change in the price of materials. One of the best strategies for dealing with these phenomena is to ensure that the project has a 'contingency element' to its budget. These extra funds must be robust in order to deal with a range of potential problems and issues. This is often a point where senior management can become uncomfortable with the amount of funding requested (contingency on top of operating budget). It should be made clear that assigning a contingency element to a project does not equate to extra liquidity that the parent organisation will never see again. A contingency is there for emergencies or dealing with changes and variations – it may not have to be used at all – so any funds allocated in this way can easily be repatriated to the organisation post project completion.

Any project – be it large or small – is (or should be) driven by its schedule. As a project progresses through its lifecycle (discussed in a later chapter), there are different and varying levels of resource requirements that come into play. A delay in schedule – regardless of the reason – will almost always result in an accruement of expenses and therefore lead to a cost overrun of some description. Schedule delays may be the result of human error or bad planning, but may also be subject to events beyond the control of the project team (e.g. a delay in fabrication by a supplier, or – as mentioned above – a rise in prices of materials and/or other inputs).

The project scope or 'scoping' the project is the Achilles' heel of successful delivery. All too often it is too wide or too narrow – leading to resultant difficulties and problems from either perspective. The scope document of a project (discussed in a later chapter) should precisely define what is included in the scope of works, what is being delivered (the reason for the project) and what is excluded from the scope of works (e.g. no provision for ongoing maintenance post-handover to the client). Another associated problem with this is what is often referred to as 'scope creep' – how this frequently comes about is due to adjustments being made to the original scope as a result of inadequacies in the original scope statement/document (see points made at the start of this paragraph). Sometimes, though, the creep in the scope occurs as a result of a request for change or varia-tion in the schedule of work from the client or their representative. If handled properly, project variation or change orders represent lit-tle or no threat when they are documented and signed off by both the individual requesting the change and the project manager. When variations occur on an informal 'can you do me a favour' approach the implications can be scary and very expensive.

Perhaps point 3 (above) is the most significant from a project risk perspective – the impact of unforeseen or random events. It is here that the organisation, project manager or project team have abso-lutely no control – indeed, some of these types of events represent uninsurable risks (floods, earthquakes, wars) and are often referred to in contracts of insurance as *force majeure* clauses. It is imperative therefore to become as fully informed as is practicable about an envi-ronment or area within which the organisation may be considering project activity.

Sometimes, though, an inverse evaluation of known or likely risks can in themselves uncover or define project opportunities – organisations that specialise in post-conflict or post-disaster reconstruction projects often possess a capability to be first on the ground to provide important services in areas ravaged by natural disaster or war. A prudently identified scope change or variation order (in the latter if agreed upon by the client) could well lead to a positive impact upon a project's financial resources, perhaps identifying an entirely new operational methodology that is more cost effective.

It is not unheard of for an organisation to capitalise on being present within an area that has allowed it to grasp a previously unforeseen opportunity by way of an entirely new project – one of the main strengths of modern corporate entities is the 'limitation field' a project can impose upon a foray into the unknown (discussed at length earlier in the book).

As operating environments become increasingly subject to change and therefore to uncertainty, a major source of increasing competitive advantage is having both the knowledge and experience to capitalise on opportunities as they present themselves – often both this knowledge and experience is distilled from previous project endeavours, i.e. the utilisation of the 'lessons learnt' doctrine (collection/collation of information and data relative to the project planning, execution and delivery phases). The proactive organisation will be quick to realise that by possessing this information and therefore having a competitive advantage over other entities that are perhaps not so experienced or knowledgeable can lead to new business and therefore to an enhancement of corporate revenue and reputation relative to its peers within a given competitive environment. The ability to capitalise in this manner is likely (as long as the organisation remains focused and does not become complacent) to have direct implications for the sustainability of a direct competitive advantage.

THE PROJECT LIFECYCLE

3

As with many things, projects have a lifecycle. The simplest representation of this idea is as follows: they are conceptual ideas – they become reality – they finish. There are many ramifications to a 'lifecycle,' some of the more obvious being that the nature of what is happening within a particular part of the lifecycle is representative of a change in both activity and the consumption of assigned resources. There are a number of commonly accepted models of project lifecycles but, to be honest, the lifecycle could be represented in any way that someone wished – there is not some universal 'written-in-stone' lifecycle structure. It is suggested, though, that whatever representation or structure is chosen, it is capable of reflecting the complexity of the project in question. So, a project lifecycle could be said to have a start, a middle and a finish and these could be the terms used to represent the lifecycle in its very simplest form.

In the upstream exploration and production sector (E&P) within the global oil industry, the most common methodology utilised for representing the project lifecycle is what is referred to as EPC (engineering, procurement and construction), so it follows that post initiation phase the engineering work is conducted, the designs are finalised and the required amount of materials and other resources are defined. Following on from this stage, the identified requisite amounts of materials, etc. are procured. Once the materials are ready the construction begins. This is not difficult to understand, though in reality many projects of this type pose significant engineering challenges and are large capital-intensive projects with an element of high risk. It is worthy of note to point out that the monitoring and control of the project lifecycle's activities should be operating at the

DOI: 10.4324/9781003188964-4

same time – distinct, continuous and detailed – across all phases. Placing the project lifecycle within a wider, more general context, another common approach is to break down the lifecycle into four distinct phases: initiation, planning, execution and close out. These will be discussed in more detail in due course.

As has been established thus far, projects themselves are often utilised as a foray into the unknown, a departure from core competencies, something new and untried for an organisation. It is important to remember that although projects may be similar to one another (i.e. the same 'type' of project: e.g. rig construction), no two projects will ever be exactly the same – different individuals may be involved, the environment may have changed, there may have been new breakthroughs in technology, etc. Therefore a critical aspect of the project lifecycle might be the inclusion or addition of an additional step or phase – namely a process for collecting, collating and analysing information post project in order to derive knowledge from the project's activities. The importance of this cannot be understated – learning what works and what doesn't is of inestimable value to an organisation: it increases efficiency, reduces cost, can enhance corporate reputation and ultimately turn the tap on new revenue streams. Some organisations elect to commence this process during the 'close-out' phase, while others prefer to conduct this review process once the project has been completed and handed over to the end user and/or client.

One of the best ways to derive maximum value from managing this knowledge would be to introduce a further step into the project lifecycle – a pre-initiation 'inception phase.' This would be an analysis of the collective store of information and knowledge based on lessons learnt and experience gained against the conceptual ideas for a new project. This can be very powerful and well worth the time invested. It serves to further refine a particular concept or idea and, if you will, can act as a filter removing those ideas or concepts that prove to be flawed or unsuitable in some manner, when measured against what is known to work, or where possible pitfalls might lie.

There are some components that are necessary if the 'inception' phase is going to add value to project performance and ultimately to successful delivery. As practically every project (or every type or 'class' of project) will at some point begin with a conceptual idea, the inception phase adds value by allowing a greater scrutiny of ideas and possibilities by comparison with the store of information/knowledge and experience that the organisation is in possession of. In the immediate term, this might well prevent the further progression of ideas that possess some inherent flaw – thereby refining time spent in conceptual development and option selection. Conclusions that begin to become defined, that take shape, should be thought of as information that can be used to make initial judgements and recommendations pre business case. Indeed, the inception process can reflect direct benefits by a pre-business case evaluation scenario – once more imparting more consistency, clarity and realism into the business case proper for a selected project.

The inception phase then should be considered as the adoption of a 'holistic' viewpoint – in that a greater range of data and information is assessed against potential project options – throughout its (the project's) entire lifespan. This focus adds real value across multiple project interfaces both internal and external. There are three further elements to a successful inception review of a potential project. While the inclusion of this mechanism serves primarily to map conceptual ideas against the known experience and knowledge thus far accumulated by the organisation, this is the time to indulge in creativity, to embed a fluidity into operational processes, to explore different angles. It is sometimes a regrettable oversight in human beings that information and knowledge within their possession is taken as read. Sometimes a breakthrough process or radical methodology is staring us in the face. We don't see it though, as we are often guilty of not analysing the information at our disposal from a different or unique perspective.

Silver bullet: An 'inception phase' must be highly creative and embed fluidity into project operational phases.

Consider the following example.

There are two companies: A and B. Both of them have decided that they wish to 'forward integrate' from manufacturing pipes to actually winning work to lay pipelines for clients. Company A has managed an entry into this marketplace, having successfully delivered a number of sub-sea pipelines as well as one large pipeline project in the same region. Company B, while a bigger entity, has yet to actually lay any form of pipeline at all. As this is a purely hypothetical scenario we can bend reality a little for the purposes of making the point.

Both A and B bid for and secure two separate pipeline-laying contracts that are to all intents and purposes identical. They are both the same type of pipeline and they are both within the same geographical region. Apart from their own product, they will both utilise the same supply chain for other resource requirements.

Company A has a 'pre-initiation' inception mechanism within its project lifecycle planning. Company B does not. Company B has conducted a reasonable level of research and is satisfied at the end of the initiation phase that they will be able to meet the deliverables of the project on time, within the required budget (so as to make a profit) and to the correct standard of specifications (the quality dimension). They have made a series of assumptions – but they do not believe that any of them are unrealistic. Both of the projects commence and progress at roughly the same speed – on schedule and without any problems of note. However, the following week two events dramatically interrupt progress. The first of these is that it begins to rain heavily – while slightly unseasonable, it is not a major surprise. Large tracts of site turn into a quagmire, significantly hampering machinery operations and movement. Coupled to this a special adhesive anti-corrosion coating that must be placed on the welds between every joint will not set if it is wet or the surface that it is to be applied to is wet. Company A learnt this lesson the previous year when they bid and won their first land pipeline job. They have a quantity of special mats nearby that are easily portable and provide a stable operating platform for heavier machinery – with the result that this machinery does not sink into the mud. They also ensured that they procured portable 'tents' that can be erected over pipe welds – allowing the welds in question to be dried out, then coated. Company B on the other hand was caught completely by surprise be these two unforeseen factors – having no contingency in place. Furthermore, when Company A had first learnt about both the mats and the tents they discovered that they came from a single specialist supplier of such materials and that there was a one-month lead time from order to delivery.

The end result? Company A completed their project on time, within budget and to the client's specifications. Company B fell about five weeks behind schedule, incurred liquidated damage penalties (LDCs) for the delay, and subsequently faced further legal action when it was discovered by third-party inspectors that the special adhesive had not bonded properly on some welds on the pipeline due to the presence of moisture. Company A went on to establish itself within this market; Company B withdrew. Although I have kept this scenario deliberately simplistic, it nevertheless serves to impart the advantages of knowledge and experience within project situations. A simple historical example: Why did Hitler invade Russia and be caught unprepared for the winter as well as the Russian's 'scorched earth' policy? Exactly the same thing had happened to Napoleons armies! Knowledge can be exploited and be a major game changer – even if it is the experience of others (which is why experienced-based learning and the resultant knowledge is closely guarded as much as possible, since it can be a direct source of competitive advantage as shown by the example above).

A real strength of the project lifecycle approach – regardless of the 'form' of a particular model – is that it directly aids clarity in a number of critically important project functions. As mentioned earlier, different activities within different stages of the project lifecycle will require changes in both quantities and types of resources that must be available. The project lifecycle supports this by providing a framework of what is happening within a particular project. This then serves to link directly with the scheduling function – often allowing planners/schedulers the ability to understand both independent and interdependent activities that are or will be taking place. Ultimately the information mentioned thus far directly benefits the project planning and control function.

THE PROJECT INITIATION PHASE

The true value of having a pre-initiation inception stage or phase discussed over the last few pages is that, if performed correctly, it will save a significant amount of time in the initiation phase as much of the background conceptual 'homework' will have been completed, allowing clarity on moving forward. It is during the project initiation phase that some of the fundamental questions should be capable of receiving coherent answers, namely: 'What are the goals and objectives of the project?' 'What is the reason for this project?' 'What is this project going to ultimately deliver?' It is important to stress here that the idea of the 'inception' stage is that it allows those involved to think on the creative level. This is where techniques such as brainstorming (in the author's opinion) hold their greatest credence – this is where all the metaphorical rocks can be lifted, peered under and preliminary conclusions and observations drawn. There are several key components to this entire activity, the first being the idea of the encouragement of creative thought, leading (hopefully) to a holistic viewpoint – not entirely dissimilar to a strategic one, though perhaps slightly more unformed or rougher around the edges. It should be noted that the conduct of this series of activities, if performed seriously and in detail, will have a significant 'fit' or influence over any strategic direction that the organisation may be seeking to take. It is here that it is important to explore possibilities (not options – that is a more refined process that belongs in the project initiation phase proper), to be fluid and consider all ideas generated, at least in the first instance.

Following on from this 'inception phase,' the primary initial focus once key possibilities and options have been identified and short-listed is to be examined and refined in more detail during the initiation phase in order to assess feasibility. Although it seems at odds with the general conversation, an option that is always available in situations where an organisation is attempting to set strategy has several (if not multiple) options and choices before them, and recognises that there is always going to be a constraining factor as to the amount and/or availability of resources that can be levied/allocated to a project is to do nothing. Sometimes, when reviewing options in the cold light of day and being utterly, ruthlessly objective, the choice not to embark upon a particular course of action might well be the wisest.

Like all things though, to achieve such clarity and objectiveness is easier said than done. Powerful organisational figures might well be driving a particular project concept forward – there might well be competing interests and agendas (as well as potential projects): everyone wants to champion their 'pet.' When this situation arises it can lead to serious complications and time wasting in project selection during the initiation phase. It should be remembered that within the project lifecycle it is the initiation phase or stage that is the vehicle for beginning the critical evaluation process of which project should be chosen. This then all too often denigrates into an utterly subjective process, where rational consideration is not given the amount of attention that it should be. All organisations are humanistic systems and because of this they do not always behave rationally, and organisational 'politics' and the nature of power will often be the deciding factors. This is discussed later on in more detail when we talk about the concept of the 'project sponsor.'

The overarching point to the project initiation phase is, in the author's opinion (in light of the comments above) to attempt to arrive at an understanding of the possible value of embarking upon a particular project. What is the project attempting to achieve? What are its objectives? What are the benefits to be gained as a result of the successful project delivery to the organisation? This is very important, as not all of these benefits will be easily measured or quantifiable – they may be tangible, easy to understand or they may be intangible.

It would be a mistake to make the assumption that the overriding reason for an organisation wishing to embark upon a project that is representative of a change of some description is solely about revenue generation and profit maximisation to the shareholders. Today, with increasing pressure upon organisations to be socially responsible and finding themselves under ever closer scrutiny by the media and the public, a project might well be selected for its benefit in terms of reputational enhancement to the organisation rather than some amount of revenue to be generated and garnered.

This type of rationale falls within the ambit of 'corporate governance' or 'corporate social responsibility' (CSR), and 'project governance' should be considered as an important subset representing the organisation's overall intentions, strategies and plans within this area. It is important to understand that not all costs and benefits are immediately (or easily) apparent and measurable. A healthy bottom line resultant from a project shows with absolute clarity the benefit to the organisation, whereas the cost of alienating people from the company and its products/services through bad publicity is uncertain (but likely to be of far more significant impact).

Although somewhat outside the parameters (and purpose) of this book, nevertheless it is important to have a fundamental understanding of CSR and what it represents to both organisation and environment. A robust set of policies within this area is a critical element for effective stakeholder management. The twin strands of identifying who the stakeholders are as well as being aware of or informed as to what their particular agendas might be are often crucial underpinnings to the project business case. We will discuss this in more detail later in the book but suffice to say it is worthy of comment at this particular juncture. Simply put, a project business case comes into being during the project initiation stage or phase and its main purpose is to answer two questions – the first being what is the rationale for the project (i.e. why would/should the organisation consider embarking upon the project – Has an opportunity been identified? Is there a threat to the organisation? Does this project provide a vehicle for maximising our competitive advantage? Will it produce new revenue streams by creating an entry into a new market?) Second, the business case serves to provide the justification for a project (i.e. What are the benefits to be realised?). As discussed above, they could be tangible in terms of enhanced revenue streams or they could be other, non-monetary benefits to the organisation such as enhanced reputation. The linkage between stakeholder management and project concept is thus exposed as being directly interlinked to ultimate project success.

Most modern definitions of what a 'project' is will include some reference or wording to 'sequence of events' or 'defined series of activities' and of course this is perfectly true. But the author feels that it is of even greater value to consider projects and their management as consisting of two different (yet equally important) strands: the physical (tangible) deliverables (i.e. the delivery of the finished product or item – for instance, a new semi-submersible drill rig) that was the reason for the project and the intangible benefits that may not be immediately apparent (a competitive advantage of some form, reputational enhancement; entry into a new marketplace, etc.) awareness of these two distinct yet often non-mutually exclusive concepts are key integral components of any robust business case. The clarity that this approach imparts will therefore contribute directly to the understanding of what the scope of the project actually is (discussed later), but will be fundamental in establishing operating parameters, what the project is supposed to be delivering (i.e. its *raison d'être)* as well as what will be excluded from the project's operations. This is a very important area within the field of project management and the author is truly amazed at how often project scoping activities go wrong (we will discuss this in more detail later in the book).

Considering the discussion thus far regarding the elements of the project initiation phase, another key aspect to add is that this phase of the project lifecycle will supply direct information as to what levels of resources are likely to be required and when. The 'when' is a crucial element (discussed in the following section). If the initiation phase of a possible project is conducted thoroughly, then key information should allow for better planning – thereby increasing the chances of project success.

Silver bullet: The project initiation phase will inform the level of resources required.

THE PROJECT PLANNING PHASE

A key element of this stage of the project lifecycle is the planning of known or likely variation in resource requirements during the different phases as the project progresses. This will allow for a greater degree of accuracy and understanding in terms of impact upon the budget, overall project performance, as well as ensuring that the allocation and mobilisation of equipment; materials and manpower is expedited in the optimum manner.

Often, the timing of when investment is required during the project lifecycle is a significant decision-making factor. There are a number of reasons as to why this is so. First, an organisation (like an individual) will only possess a finite amount of resources. The key question for an organisation considering any form of investment is going to formulate its decision-making process around several key criteria, of which when and how much capital is going to be required ranks among the most important. The level of risk and therefore uncertainty facing the organisation is going to be balanced against the possible return and rewards should the project prove successful. The degree of acceptance (of this relationship) (i.e. how much risk is permissible/acceptable) will in large part be down to the culture of the organisation and the attitude towards risk of its strategic decision makers. Operationally, a project option that may hypothetically require a steady 'drip feed', or a constant incremental injection of cash at regular intervals, may place less of a strain on the organisation's normal day-to-day activities (remember that often a project represents a journey into the unknown for the organisation – success is seldom a given). For another organisation that has built up a 'war chest' and has a source of available investment liquidity, a project that requires a greater amount of investment towards the front end may be a more attractive option (gain a 'first-mover advantage' over competitors who may not be in such a financially strong position). Perhaps the project option that requires most of the investment in the later stages of the project lifecycle is the best one for either the organisation with the financial resources or the one hoping to exploit some form of future cash flow.

All of these considerations demonstrate the sometimes complex nature of making project investment decisions and serve to highlight why deployment of financial resources may not be a simple linear process. It is with this discussion in mind that we can become better informed regarding a significant proportion of the underlying rationale and reasoning for the project planning phase.

By way of imparting a useful structure to the reader, let us discuss some of the other salient parts of the project planning phase one at a time.

1 The creation of a detailed operational structure

The purpose of this component of the planning stage is to attempt to rationalise 'how' the execution phase is going to achieve its objectives (i.e. the project 'deliverables'). This is therefore an exercise is creating an 'architecture.' The first element of this process is to examine the human dimension. It is imperative that the required individuals are identified at this stage. Reporting lines, ownership and task accountability need to be established and clearly understood here by all parties concerned. Projects are often complex, interactive endeavours operating in a dynamic environment – the number of interfaces is potentially very large. Attention to these areas where 'contact' or overlap occurs is a significant element of importance for project planners, not least of all from a stakeholder management perspective.

A logical, methodical approach is the best way to achieve success in this element of the project planning phase. I have always found it highly effective when planning the implementation (execution) of operational activities to break the overall 'event' into discreet, progressive 'chunks' or pieces. This 'staged' approach allows for more accurate awareness and understanding of what might be required in 'real time.'

2 Control and review mechanisms established

The next step in the process is to look to further augment the human element established above. The planning process should now shift its attention to the establishment of control mechanisms by which ownership, accountability and reporting structures become crystallised or solidified within the planning documentation (i.e. an agreed-upon, defined mechanism). The approach here needs to be from a dual perspective. As well as the above-mentioned aspects, it is of paramount importance that all review mechanisms for the evaluation of a project's performance (both in human performance and actual project performance terms) are built into the architecture at this juncture to ensure that there is absolute clarity in both the subject and the manner of review.

3 Information management

Projects are team endeavours and, as mentioned above, operate across a variety of interfaces and are subject to the attentions of a multitude of stakeholders. For these reasons, the author recommends that project information be managed around the 'SMART' criteria (i.e. information that is specific, measurable, accurate, reliable and timeous). The dissemination of information of this type should not be circulated exclusively internally to the project team and organisational members but should also seek to inform stakeholder interests that lie externally to both the project and the parent organisation. In addition to this aspect, the relevance (and therefore the value) of information generated, collected and collated during the project lifecycle should seek to inform – therefore it should be capable of being understood by relevant parties. A key role of the control methodology mentioned in

(2) above is to ensure that this type of understanding is facilitated across all associated boundaries and parties. Information is also the key to both creating and managing the expectations that arise for a project from the stakeholder groupings. Unrealistic or unfeasible expectations – if not managed with due attention – can lead to serious problems at some future point either during the project execution (or possibly worse) post project performance. The end goal of the information management process is to ensure that value is added through its (the information's) availability, dissemination and rationalisation to add value to the project delivery process.

Silver bullet: Information is a primary and very valuable resource. It is a direct factor in whether or not a competitive advantage exists for the organisation within its (the organisation's) chosen marketplace. Commensurate with its value, it must be managed and controlled very carefully. Confidential information should only be possessed by those duly authorised within either the organisation or the project team.

4 Assignment of allocated resources

Every project manager knows that any given project is going to suffer from resource constraints of some sort at some point during its lifecycle. As projects tend to be bound by the triumvirate of the 'iron triangle' (delivered on time, within budget, to the required quality) (mentioned earlier), the effective allocation of budgeted resources is a centrally important operational process for which to plan. The assignment process mapped out here during the planning phase is critical to ensure operational fluidity. It is therefore an imperative function of project planning to ensure that the tasks required to complete work packages and the collective completion of work packages themselves towards the overall deliverables of the project are assigned the required level of resources. This is a deterministic process and it can be difficult to remove subjectivity – experience is worth its weight in gold at this juncture. Assignment of resources also has a secondary attribute – it is the best way to track the efficiency of performance and progress, both from a personnel and material consumption perspective.

5 Contingency allocations

When considering point (4) above, the concept of contingency allocations should be very much at the fore of the project planner's mind. Planning and the plans that are created should never be viewed as 'set in stone'; the environmental turbulence within which the modern corporate entity finds itself operating – increasing technological acceleration, shifting (even fleeting) periods of competitive advantage, the possibility of new entrants at any moment given the growth in globalisation – all point to the need for flexibility and the capability to adapt to a fluid situation. Effective contingency allocations are a major means to this end. Contingency allocations tend to get 'sticky' – the financial and accounting functions do not necessarily welcome assignment of 'extra' funds to a project budget. It is imperative that those involved in the resourcing of a project make it absolutely clear that the contingency budgets may never be used (all being well) – but, from a time and delivery perspective, should the need arise to deal with a resource issue it can be dealt with (in most cases) immediately by drawing upon contingency funds.

THE PROJECT EXECUTION PHASE

This is the part of the project where physical work begins in order to achieve the desired deliverables. Resources begin to be consumed as work commences – starting with the actual mobilisation of the operational requirements in order to deliver the project. It must be borne in mind, though, that although resources have been identified (and in the case of 'human resources' authorised) as project components, the reality, as with so many things, may often prove more difficult. In order to ensure that the resources planned for physically arrive, it is suggested that the project manager ensures the close support of the project sponsor or steering committee. It is often the case that a particular project finds itself in competition for resources with other projects. The more directly involved (at this juncture) the senior management support is, the more likely the project will receive the planned resource and budgetary allocations. Another place where this support is invaluable is when it comes to establishing reporting lines and responsibility. If a key individual is going to be 'loaned' to a project, this can quite often be a 'non-desirable' event for a departmental or functional line manager. Conflicts and problems can and do arise where a functional manager is a more senior organisational figure than the project manager; hence once more the influence and support of the project sponsor become relevant – being able to step in and mitigate such situations by using their position and power.

It is probably better in these situations to see whether the 'loaned' individual can be transferred across to the project full time for its duration rather than part time. Among other aspects, this will allow the individual to focus exclusively on the project and not be distracted by the requirements of their 'normal' job.

The mobilisation of project resources is often a chaotic time. There are many different activities requiring coordination and control and, all too often, a degree of organisational inertia must be overcome in order to get things moving. What this demonstrates is just how great the variety of challenges facing the project manager are from day one.

As activity escalates and allocated resources begin to be consumed, it becomes imperative that monitoring and control mechanisms are activated in order to gauge the overall progress and performance of the project. These mechanisms serve as the first line of defence by providing an 'early warning' should progress or resource consumption begin to deviate from the established plan or target. If this is the case, then questions should be raised and action taken to correct or realign the project direction – to put the project 'back on track' so to speak.

One of the optimum methodologies of ensuring an efficient project execution is to delegate control via ownership and responsibilities to the project team – 'micromanagement' should be avoided at all costs. In order to do this effectively, it makes a lot of common sense to ensure that the execution of the plan is structured in order to facilitate this process. 'Breaking down' the project deliverables into sub-components such as work packages derived from the overall Work Breakdown Structure (WBS) is, in the author's opinion, the best way to do this. We will discuss WBS and work packages in due course within this book.

A point of some significance for the project manager in light of the discussion above is to identify the number of interfaces that may (and will) arise within the life of the project. Interfaces are those areas where the boundaries 'mix' or blur into one another – areas where the issue of ownership and control may become uncertain. Primary interaction with stakeholders be they internal or external occur at the interface between different activities. For instance, examples of interfaces include those between the contracts department and the procurement department, or between a supplier and the warehousing function – even a meeting with representatives of different organisational functions to discuss elements of the project. They must be managed with care and attention and monitored continually. The effective management of interfaces is a direct precursor to overall successful project delivery. They are also likely to have longer term advantages (if handled/managed properly) from the perspective of getting to know other people and organisations – it gives both the project manager and the project team the opportunity to begin to build long-lasting beneficial relationships. Communication and the ability to manage potential conflict are key aspects of successful interface management – in short dealing with other people.

A number of years ago, the author was a 'project trouble shooter' for a very large gas pipeline. One day I received a phone call from a very aggressive project operations manager. This individual was aggressive in the extreme to everything and everyone that came across his path. He was a driven individual who demanded results from all those who worked for him. He didn't believe in idle chit-chat nor most societal niceties. His focus was absolute. He had been very successful in the past and without a doubt knew what he was doing. On this particular day, he was phoning me to tell me that some key supplies had just been delivered and were faulty. I phoned the supplier and introduced myself. The supplier at first didn't seem very interested in talking with me, finally revealing that he had 'been verbally abused' over the phone earlier that morning. I apologised and explained what the situation actually was. The reason for the faulty goods was not immediate, so we both agreed to investigate from our respective sides. I could find nothing. The problem was that if we didn't get this issue sorted out quickly, all operational activity would cease on the pipeline and it would become a litigation frenzy among the multitude of subcontractors, who would be prevented from delivering to their contractual timetables. As the situation stood, there was only a residue of the correct material (from the previous order) that was good for about five more days. The clock was ticking. The next day the supplier phoned me. He had discovered the reason for the fault: the particulate size of the material in question was at the smallest end of the range – all previous orders had contained particles at the opposite end of the specified range. Clearly there had been a mistake in the specification, as the current delivery was useless. Even as the supplier spoke and told me that they were not to blame and had no case to answer, I was thinking that this wasn't going to end well. In the next sentence, the supplier told me that he had been impressed by my attitude and calmness in dealing with a crisis and he had enjoyed working with me in this investigation. He did not hold me responsible for the rude and abrasive attitude of the operations manager. The problem then, though, was that he was the only supplier in the country and brought it in with a lead time of five weeks via ship. At this point we had four days left.

The supplier informed me that this problem was taken care of – he had organised another load with the larger particulate size and it was being trucked up to the project front end as we spoke and should arrive within 36 hours (which it did). Furthermore, the supplier said that there would be no charge and they would simply 'swop' the loads of materials – taking away the earlier quantity that had been delivered. A crisis had been averted – not due to anything clever, but probably due to a dose of good luck and most definitely due to attitude and communication. The stakeholder relationship interface can produce miracles if managed properly.

In addition, failure to manage interfaces correctly has a lot of negative connotations for a project – performance may slip, leading to wasted consumption of resources and negative budgetary impact as costs overrun. Another resource that no project can ever afford to squander is time – if resources (as mentioned above) are consumed inefficiently or wastefully, then the spectre of rework looms large, or perhaps some other form of corrective action. The consequence of such a requirement is the consumption of extra time. This in itself will lead to problems such as schedule slippage/delay – a 'ripple' or 'knock-on' effect that is likely to impact on the overall timing to completion and delivery of the project. To prevent this, it may become necessary to 'crash' activities within a certain component of the project schedule – at an additional premium cost in order to 'reclaim' the lost time and set the schedule back on track.

CLOSE OUT

As mentioned in the preceding paragraph, although a project is a finite endeavour, responsible individuals should always be looking towards the future horizon – establishing long-term relationships across the various interfaces with the different stakeholder groupings and interests is a certain way to maximise the future potential (and ease) of upcoming projects. Established 'interface protocols' create the path for continued beneficial relationships, making it easier to deal with other parties as they are no longer unknown entities. The close-out phase of any project is obviously representative of a critical element of this entire process. Once the project has been delivered, the importance of ensuring that the processes of closure and handover are completed in a thorough and timely manner cannot be over-emphasised. This is the point, to be blunt, where the customer (whoever they may be) is satisfied. From the external perspective this translates into whether or not any future business will be generated. A messy, inefficient project close out can create a lasting negative impression – to be avoided at all costs.

Silver bullet: Established 'interface protocols' create the path for continued beneficial relationships, making it easier to deal with other parties as they are no longer 'unknown entities' once these protocols are 'activated for the first time.'

There are four significant steps to an effective project close out. They are as follows:

1   Scope compliance/achievement
2   Contractual/administrative close out
3   Lessons learnt review
4   Knowledge capture – experience/learning

1 Scope compliance/achievement

Many projects end up over budget, suffering from a quality issue or late due to 'mis-scoping.' The scope documentation of a project should precisely define what a project exists to achieve (i.e. what its deliverables are), as well as what the agreed exclusions are (i.e. what is not included in the project's scope of work). For some reason, though, this tends to be a part of the project that is often handled badly – either the scope tends to be too wide and therefore includes extra activities and costs, or tends towards being too narrow – with the result that important aspects of the deliverables are not included and accounted for early on in the project planning stage. Another common malaise that afflicts the process of 'scoping' a project is what is known as 'scope creep'. This tends to happen when the deliverables of a project are 'tweaked' or modified in some manner – culminating collectively into a departure of some significance.

Although it is (in all reality) too late at close out to realise a mistake in the scope of a project, there are two points to make here. First, recognise the potential position in which you might find yourself when you have to delay the close out and expected handover to the client. That in itself bodes ill for both you as an individual, the project team and your organisation in a wider sense. If possible litigation is looming, or in fact liquidated damage clauses (LDCs) swing into operation you are not going to be very popular to say the least. It is always worth running through a mental checklist of 'close-out possibilities' at the start of a project so that you're not caught napping.

Second, should the above come to pass you will have to deal with it. Other issues aside, the true value here is to learn from your mistakes. Understand what went wrong, what went right and why things transpired in the manner that they did. This is discussed in more detail below.

If, on the other hand, it becomes apparent at close out that the scope has been 'achieved,' then it is fairly safe to say (all things being equal) that the project will be considered a success by all concerned. The hard-won kudos are yours and the team's – well done. The same thing applies though in this situation as that discussed from the negative perspective above: analyse why the project was a success and identify what was good and what was bad – enough said. This will be discussed in more detail below.

2 Contractual/administrative close out

There is an old adage that states: 'No job is properly completed until the paperwork is done.' This is never truer than during the close-out phase of a project. From the administrative perspective, this is the time to ensure that the final discharge of reports, tasks associated with ownership and responsibility and any other form of stakeholder interaction are completed and documented for audit purposes. Documents should be collected, collated and archived (once any 'lessons learnt'-type information has been extracted for future use). The administrative close-out procedure therefore provides a useful verification methodology in ensuring that the project has delivered what it set out to do and that all stakeholders (both internal and external) have had their expectations satisfied. Closing out this stage properly sends a clear, unequivocal message to all concerned that the project is over and complete.

3 Lessons learnt/review

Arguably, the success of this stage or phase is the most important in terms of the potential impact on future business (projects). Any possible flaws and/or weaknesses in documentary control and procedures as well as anything at fault within the contractual process can be identified and rectified from a 'lessons learnt' perspective – and therefore not repeated. In the author's experience, this process tends to suffer from one inherent weakness, namely a lack of continuity in capturing (or indeed applying at a later date) the 'story' of the project's performance (i.e. what went right and what went wrong). Too often 'lessons learnt' are nothing more than a 'bundling' of technical data representing some history of a project's lifecycle. For example, a while ago, the author was hired as a consultant to look to find ways to integrate the supply chain function with the project function of a large international organisation. When I asked to see the lessons learnt documentation, I received a very large number of spreadsheets detailing all the purchase orders, fabrication lead times of key components, quality specifications and expected date of delivery. This, in my opinion, is not what a 'lessons learnt' documentation pack should consist of. Think about this for a moment. Undoubtedly, there is a significant amount of relevant and pertinent information contained therein but it does not represent a distillation of any facts – it tells no story. The story – once supporting information has been collected, analysed and collated – provides the vehicle for guidance for future project endeavours. This brings us to our next and final stage of the project close-out procedure – the capturing of knowledge and the reflection of learning and experience gained.

4 Knowledge capture, experience and learning

There is an increasing realisation in the corporate world of today that knowledge must be captured – that experience gained and learning that takes place as a result of this process is ultimately the source of creating a sustainable competitive advantage. Note that I use the word 'sustainable' in relation to competitive advantage. Why? Well, conventional thought used to dictate that an organisation would arrive at a point in the market where they enjoyed some form of advantage that gave them a competitive edge such as proprietary technology, control of distribution channels or being a single-source supplier. The business environment of today, however, is in a state of flux. What this means for the corporate entities engaged within competitive business is that any advantage is likely to be time bound and not perpetual or even (quite often) long lasting. In business environments where change is the singular constant the critical question must be: At what rate must we change? Note that implicit within this question is the realisation that the organisation cannot afford to stand still – that it recognises that it must change in order to survive and remain competitive. The crux of the 'change paradigm' is, as stated above, to change at the right speed. Conventional wisdom dictates that if an organisation was to 'change' or evolve away from its core competencies (i.e. what it is good at, what it is known for, where it competes, etc., that is to say, change too rapidly) into different markets, it will more than likely alienate its core customers. Many are the organisations that thought a loyal customer base ensured an ongoing competitive advantage. This simple truth might be better understood by the realisation, in most cases, that customers will be loyal as long as it suits them. This is why the organisation must be proactive and change in order to match the anticipations of both the market and the consumer/customer.

Conversely, should the organisation fail to change enough, then market dynamics will dictate that it (the company) is likely to be left behind – perhaps by becoming uncompetitive in price and/or service; perhaps for failing to capitalise on market opportunities, or being slow to react to new market entrants with new products and technologies. This happens on a daily basis. This is why, increasingly, organisations are turning to the project methodology in order to achieve efficient change – it grants a modicum of flexibility and limits risk to the extent of time/money/resources allocated. It thus becomes imperative that the organisation is able to assess the rate of change within its operating environments, as this will have a direct impact on the above discussion. From my personal perspective, I believe that there are two fundamental questions that must be addressed by the organisation. First, whether or not the organisation possesses the capability to change – many in number are those corporate entities that stick to the mantra: 'If it isn't broke, don't fix it.' While this does make sense to a limited degree it will be a death sentence in the longer term. Second, if the organisation could change, does it possess the resources required? It's a bit like cosmetic surgery – yep, I'd like to change this and that but I can't afford it, so nothing happens. This is exactly the same from the corporate perspective.

Another significant dimension to pay definite attention to is to recognise the power and value inherent within the organisation's ability to harness learning – be it from either a positive (i.e. what worked), or a negative (what didn't) perspective, and to utilise this collected experience for moving forward – for activation of the legal principle of '*mutatis mutandis*' (i.e. 'change that which must be changed'). It has always baffled the author that in times of cost cutting, downsizing and streamlining, the organisation seems to consciously decide upon the very destructive path of removing those individuals with the most experience and knowledge, keeping instead the younger crop of 'rising stars', who will not rise too high without a wise mentor and knowledgeable guide. What is an inescapable truth is that any organisation's ability to operate, to compete, to be a market benchmark is ultimately encapsulated within the knowledge of its employees. In the sense of the project management sphere, it is this recognition of the collective talents and abilities of the project team by the project manager that separates the high-performing project from the over-budget/out-of-time also rans.

Knowledge, learning and experience are best captured and utilised through open and effective dialogue – with communication spreading information throughout the organisation. This is easily said. Why, then, does it appear to be so fundamentally problematic to achieve? The author would suggest that the answer lies within the nature of organisations themselves. Corporate systems are humanistic systems, in that the 'will' of the corporate entity is in fact the will of those who make the decisions on behalf of the organisation. All humanistic systems are fundamentally flawed in that behaviour by individuals is never perfectly objective in terms of decision making if we were to be honest. Organisational politics – 'power-plays' and emotive responses in terms of likes and dislikes of one another – should really be recognised as the corporate cancer that destroys companies from the inside out. This entire behavioural pattern is often seen in an even more exacerbated form post-merger or acquisition transaction, hence the reason that the majority of M&A transactions do not have a happy ending – despite an absolutely rational and value-adding synergy created on paper by what each of the parties 'brings to the table.'

THE PROJECT MANAGER

Let us take a moment to sum up the basic components of what a project is and what it exists to do. Normally of a defined duration (i.e. it will last 'X' long (days, weeks, months, years)), etc., it exists for a defined purpose (i.e. to 'deliver' something) (to achieve something). The mechanism of delivery is through the actions of a team of functional specialists, each carrying out assigned tasks (the project team). Projects have a defined amount of resources (finance, materials, etc.) which will be consumed throughout the defined duration in accordance with a plan and a schedule at different rates as per the project lifecycle (discussed below). Projects also have a leader – the conductor of the orchestra so to speak – the project manager (PM).

This is where it gets interesting. No project that the author has ever heard of succeeded with a bad project team – alternatively some projects still deliver, even with a bad or incompetent PM, but more often than not they are late and/or significantly over budget.

Silver bullet: The very essence of project management is about the management and leadership of a team of other people who are specialists in defined areas of expertise who are contributing towards a common goal or purpose.

There is a vital point to highlight here though: the project manager is (and must be) a part of the team. The author often despairs when he hears a PM say that they are 'not part of the project team – the project team works for me.' This is a dangerous and counter-productive

DOI: 10.4324/9781003188964-5

attitude to have – if the PM is going to deliver a project successfully they are only going to do it with the help of their team.

The author would suggest that what has to happen for a project to succeed is for the PM to achieve the 'buy-in' from the project team (i.e. the belief (from the project team) in the skills and leadership abilities of the PM). So what skills should a project manager have? The first statement that the author would make is that the skills required conform to the 'double-V' rule – that they are both vast and varied. The author believes that this skillset can be broken down into two components. First, those skills and abilities that allow other processes to occur, and second, the management and guidance of such processes. The first category of skills would encapsulate the following: the PM would have superb communication abilities; would naturally build relationships with others; would manage and prevent conflict within both the project team itself and/or the wider environment; would have empathy and therefore understanding of the positions and perspectives of others, and would be creative and imaginative in solving problems.

Silver bullet: The 'critical success factor' for any project is the team 'buy-in' of the PM's leadership and abilities.

The second category of skills would consist of the 'control' or 'oversight' of some of the following characteristics: the ability to coach, enforce, control and motivate those individuals within the project team and to be closely engaged with them (the project team).

Let us take the opportunity now to examine these categories of skills in more detail – beginning with the first category. The first essential skill that anyone who wishes to be considered, or considers themselves to be a successful project manager, is that of communicative ability. Given the nature of the project environment, both the necessity and nature of communication is amplified due to the uncertainties and expectation of performance. There are often a multitude of stakeholders to be managed, all with differing levels of power, interest and impact/influence upon the project. We will examine stakeholders in more detail in due course. Given this dynamic, it becomes imperative then that the PM is able to express concepts with great clarity – ensuring that everyone is on the same page, so to speak. Many projects have a strong international element – they are likely to either be operating within a different cultural environment, or the project team itself may be composed of individuals representing different stakeholders and national interests or may simply be a mixture of people across a range of cultures. Either way, when considering multicultural interfaces, where people have different values and beliefs, the scope for miscommunication is greatly amplified. Coupled very strongly with the ability to speak and express oneself effectively and clearly is the ability to listen carefully. If truth be told, most of us are not good listeners when other people are speaking. This was summed up very succinctly many years ago by a drill sergeant when the author was in the army. He said: 'You have two of these', gesturing to his ears, 'and one of these', gesturing to his mouth. 'Therefore, you should do twice as much listening as speaking.' We got the message, and I have never forgotten it. Another critical skill is that of attitude. Now this might sound strange, but the reader may recall that I mentioned earlier about those PMs one meets who do not consider themselves to be part of the project team – this is the starting point for disaster. So, what about attitude? As I stated earlier, project management is quite simply managing a team of individuals who have specialist skills and are working collectively towards the delivery of a defined objective. But the project environment is often uncertain at best and the scope for change or impacting events upon the project's performance is very wide indeed. People are strange creatures. One of the things people really like is being listened to – having a voice, having an opinion. A good PM recognises this and not only listens to the project team but is also open to ideas and suggestions as to how the performance and, ultimately, delivery of the project can be enhanced. How problems can be overcome, how adversity can be surmounted. This shows respect for the individual, who will in turn show respect for the leadership of the PM. Remember the comment about the starting point for success is the achievement of 'buy-in' by the project team members? Well, this is one of the quickest and easiest ways to achieve this and turn a bunch of people into a high-performing project team that is motivated and has a strong sense of both purpose and identity.

When teaching on the MSc. Project Management programme at the University of Aberdeen many years ago I had a most interesting 'debate' with one of the class early on within my subject which was one of the final year modules – managing project teams. As I walked up onto the dais on a Saturday morning, took my place behind my lectern and gazed at my class of hard-bitten PMs (they actually were – it was a requirement for entry into this particular programme), I thought that it was appropriate to start off with a challenging remark. 'I can manage any project in the world,' I said, meeting everyone's gaze. Sure enough, there was a student in the class who bridled instantly at this seemingly arrogant and ridiculous statement. He was an extremely experienced PM, an engineer by trade, and had over 15 years of running highly technical, big-budget, subsea engineering projects in the North Sea. I was particularly delighted that he had picked up the gauntlet – he would be a worthy opponent. He reminded me that I myself had said the previous weekend (which was our first together) that I 'wasn't a technical guy' and had no engineering experience – how then did I think that I would have a snowball in hell's chance of running an engineering-based, highly complex, big-budget, high-pressure subsea project? 'Easily,' was my immediate reply. He snorted and shook his head as if he was having trouble believing that he had to listen to this idiot at the front of the room. 'It's all to do with the project team,' I said. 'If I have the right people in my project team with the right expertise and I listen to them – the sky's the limit,' I continued, enjoying myself immensely. My colleague once more shook his head and appeared to be muttering to himself – looking slightly angry and no doubt wondering if he had subscribed to the right university programme.

I decided it was time to make my next move. I asked him that, to be sure I had understood, his stance was that to be able to run a subsea project I should not only be a fully qualified subsea engineer, I should also have the requisite amount of practical experience, knowledge and understanding of the subject matter at hand. He nodded, looking slightly more pleased. 'That's it exactly,' he said. 'Okay,' I replied, 'then I should also be a chartered accountant so that I could understand the financial aspects of the project, and I'd better be a fully qualified lawyer too so that I would be competent and knowledgeable about all of the legal ramifications of the contract documentation and any other legal issue that might arise.' The individual in question was openly staring at me. Several of his colleagues, oil and gas guys themselves, were laughing. 'I'd never thought of it like that,' he said. 'Do you understand my position now?' I asked him with what I hoped was a winning smile. 'I think I'll just keep quiet from now on,' he said, still looking very thoughtful. 'Project management is easy. It's all about the team. If you have the right people with the right knowledge then any project is deliverable – successfully.' I concluded. I am still in touch with him today – quite a few years on from his MSc. days.

This story also serves as an example of being 'open' to a new perspective – to challenge the norms, to seek new ways to achieve things. The value of this within a dynamic, high-pressure project environment is incalculable.

Another key attribute real professional PMs have is that they are slow to make assumptions. Now, the author realises that often assumptions are necessary in order to reach a conclusion or arrive at a decision, but these are assumptions that are based on some kind of supporting data or information. What I am focusing on here is the humanistic dimension (i.e. making assumptions without any basis of fact – unfortunately something most of us do far too much). I recall standing in a queue at a cash machine one afternoon at my local bank and watching different people walking towards one another. On one side we had three pretty young girls, dressed to impress, laughing and tossing their hair about – exuding that certainty that comes with youth. I've no doubt that they were either going shopping or heading off for a coffee – three friends having a good day together. Approaching them was a single man, unshaven, hair rather wild, wearing tracksuit bottoms and a T-shirt. As they passed each other, it was obvious by their giggles that the girls thought this guy was not up to much. They turned to look behind them and I must tell you – I found it highly amusing seeing the look on these young ladies' faces as the guy (who to be fair was more than a little scruffy in appearance) climbed into a Porsche 911 and drove away. I think the conclusion here is fairly self-evident.

So, we have established a number of key operating parameters for our ideal PM. We have also identified that the essence of project management is the management (via process) and the leadership (via talent and creativity) of a disparate group of individuals who possess specialist skillsets and are collectively focused towards the delivery of a given project. The author would now encourage the reader to sit back and evaluate what comes next. I have made a number of statements pertaining to this idea of being an inclusive part of the project team and that, indeed, in the author's opinion, this is the secret ingredient – the 'magical elixir' for project success. Fine. But there's more to this – and there has to be: right? Once more we find ourselves back with the human interface. The PM has to understand the people who are part of the project team. The PM must realise that individuals are just that – individual. This means that they are different. If they are different they will have different strengths and weaknesses, desires, hopes and ambitions and different abilities. The secret is to know where best to extract the maximum contribution from each and every individual so that their particular contribution is maximised for the project's favourable delivery. So, how is this achievable, you ask? Step 1 is to know your people – to know (or at least have a fairly good idea) of everyone's strengths and weaknesses – what are they good at, what are they bad at? We can further pursue this line of questioning by then asking ourselves: What is it that the individual is seeking? Are they strictly a 'comfort zone' operator, or do they thirst after challenge and achievement? You will probably find that there are both broad types of these individuals in any given project team. You, as the PM, must know how to harness these disparate streams of energy – to be the prism that focuses the effort on the maximum gain.

To go back a step: above I use the term 'comfort zone operator'. The truth is, ladies and gentlemen, that this is where the majority of people like to be. They like to be in control of what they are doing and have surety in their contribution towards the achievement of their personal role within the project team. They want to know what is expected of them and they want to execute these expectations calmly and competently. No problem: people like this are like gold dust. However, a good project team needs another ingredient – the maverick, the risk taker, the gambler – the individual who wants to push their boundaries, who wants to see if they can achieve all that they believe they could if they are given the right opportunity. You as the PM have a duty to provide these opportunities for these firebrands but to keep them under control, and – strangely enough – we find we are back at the point of 'mentoring, coaching and developing' other people. Do I need to comment further?

If we consider the two broad categories of the above-mentioned individuals (and they do cover almost everyone you will encounter on a project team), it becomes obvious that this is the foundation of the 'team dynamic'. It is vitally important to understand that humans, by their very nature, interact with one another within a given environment and it is this interaction that defines the collective group (or team identity) – its values, beliefs and normative behaviour patterns. Some people are 'strong' – outspoken, confident and (regrettably) sometimes 'bullish' towards their colleagues – while others are quieter, more introspective and prefer to stay out of the spotlight. Depending on the various temperaments, this is an area of interface that must be managed closely if it is to lead to enhanced productivity and team-based results.

Earlier on in this topic, I mentioned the phenomenon of team 'buy-in' and made the statement that this was critical to the success of both the team (in terms of productivity) and the project (in terms of delivery). We have established that this 'buy-in' will very much depend on the attitude and leadership skills of the PM. There is, however, something more that is represented by this elusive 'buy-in' factor: the question of trust. The author would suggest that this is one of the most precious commodities a human can possess. It is, however, a double-edged sword – normally we, as humans, do not trust people we do not know or that we dislike – hence, once more, I redirect you back to the idea of 'building relationships.' You have to give trust in order to receive trust – just as within any other kind of interactive relationship between people. So, any good PM would trust his team and their particular expertise. By doing this, several key benefits are realised. First, the project manager is showing his team that he recognises their competence in their particular role or field of expertise – the confidence that this inspires in the leadership of the project manager is returned by the team in turn trusting them (the PM). Second, an open approach such as this prevents the dreaded scourge of 'micro-management' – anathema to any project being successful in my most heartfelt opinion. Delegation (and this is what, de facto, the project manager is doing) is the key to a project team that is both motivated and inspired towards the end goal of the project delivery.

A basic problem with human interaction is that we are all individual and have a need (whether conscious or unconscious) to be recognised by our peers. If an individual feels that they are not receiving enough respect for what they do, or believes that someone dislikes them (the list of potential factors is actually quite long), then unfortunately that ugly spectre called conflict can begin to manifest. Conflict in a project team is not a good idea – period. Stress and conflict are inextricably linked – stress can lead to conflict and conflict may generate stress; there are no winners in this particular cycle, only collateral damage. It is important to understand that stress is a personal thing – any given group of individuals will react differently under the same circumstances, depending on their psychological make-up. I mentioned at the start of this paragraph that we are all individuals – fine – but I invite you to consider this for a moment. A human being is a lot more susceptible to nuances and influences than you might initially realise; after all, this is how advertising and marketing work – to make something appealing that might actually not be, or in the words of the professionals in the area, 'to create a demand'. Thus we are the sum product of our experiences – time and life work ceaselessly to craft and shape us all. So, individually, our values and beliefs are built upon a foundation of experiences. These experiences and what we believe to be right or wrong, acceptable or not acceptable, are all therefore based on what we have learned as we have lived and, very importantly, our perceptions of the world around us. This therefore is the key to understanding stress – it is a personal thing. Consider this. Someone who suffers from chronic arachnophobia would not like to encounter a tarantula in their tent on a camping trip somewhere exotic – imagine their reaction compared to someone who had absolutely no fear of spiders at all and thought, 'wow, look at this fella' – how lucky we are to be able to observe (and maybe hold!) a real live tarantula in its native environment. The difference, therefore, is, as already mentioned, purely down to personal perception – and this is identical when it comes to stress and the human race. Consider the Stress Causation Paradigm model shown in Figure 4.1

The important thing of note in the model shown in Figure 4.1 is that it is not in any way sequential but is rather designed to be representative of a 'cluster' effect (i.e. the outlying circle of factors are the components that create the central factor – stress). These outlying factors will be representative of different levels of impact relevant to the particular case in hand. The value of this model is that it serves to illustrate key causal factors that can be utilised to evaluate a situation or an environment – to attempt to alleviate or minimise stress to its lowest possible common denominator. There is also a lot of

Figure 4.1 The Stress Causation Paradigm model

duality in the factors as in a given situation – some of them might be 'counterbalancing' and might not be of a negative value. This model is intended to be adapted and utilised on a case-by-case basis by the particular project manager or project team as and when a situation might require an intervention of some type. The factors are all inter-linked in a 'mesh' of interconnectivity. The brief discussion that follows is simply a 'heads up' for the reader's consideration of each particular factor. The author stresses that they are not to be read as a particular factor having more importance as per the model – it will be dependent upon the case in hand.

Communication

The author believes that most of us are not effective communicators because we don't *really* listen to what the other person is saying.

People tend to 'tune out' and simultaneously 'search ahead,' thinking of other things that are happening or needing to be done – there is a loss of focus. This loss of focus can then translate into the manifestation of stress, for a whole plethora of reasons – not understanding explicit instructions; forgetting something vital and not wanting to query for clarification for fear of 'losing face', – the list is long. We've all been there and know just how damaging this can be. In the increasingly international projects of today, this problem is exacerbated cross-culturally where individuals might not possess a first-language grasp of either their spoken vocabulary, written skills or interpretation of what has been said to them.

Culture

People from different places on our planet tend to reflect different sets of normative behaviours, beliefs and ways of doing things – as well as different languages (mentioned in the previous factor). Businesses and particularly projects are now very cosmopolitan in nature. Cultural insensitivity, leading to misjudgements and possibly offence being caused, can have very grave ramifications for a project's successful delivery. When considering the previous factor, poor communication is often the point of origin of the onset of stress-related behavioural manifestations and a decline in team and/or individual motivation and productivity.

Workload

The point has been made in this book about identifying (from the PM's perspective) where the relevant 'comfort zones' lie with individual team members. In my experience one of the most significant stressors is that of workload. Far too frequently, some organisational genius will come up with the plan to save money by downsizing/ streamlining an organisation/department/function/project. How this generally plays out is in a reduction of personnel. The problem then tends to be that this reduced number of personnel are supposed to continue to manage the workload of the previous larger numbers of individuals who were engaged. Burnout and fatigue are often the end stage results of this degree of stress placed upon people. Examining this from the 'cluster' perspective of this model, it becomes easy to understand how different cultures have differing work ethics in terms of what is an acceptable workload and the performance of said workload can often be dependent upon the efficiency (or not) of communication protocols.

Uncertainty

If the reader considers the factors thus so far espoused, it is not a difficult reach to understand the interrelation and interconnectivity of the 'cluster' of stress-related factors. Poor communication across cultural boundaries, coupled with a poorly defined scope of work (workload), will all lead to uncertainty and lack of action/productivity within a project team as individuals struggle to cope while not being too sure of what it is that they are trying to achieve or are responsible for in terms of project delivery. As projects are often a foray into the unknown for the organisation, any increase in the level of uncertainty both externally (the environment) and internally (the project team) is unlikely to have a positive and productive effect.

Time

Time is the most precious of all resources and sadly, time that is lost on a project is permanently lost. If the reader considers the discussion thus far on this model, the impact of insufficient time and how this relates to all the other factors mentioned thus far should be obvious. When individuals are struggling, they are stressed – when they are stressed, they are increasingly unproductive. Unproductive/ unmotivated/disenchanted individuals will waste time – perhaps consciously or simply by way of not understanding what is happening or expected of them within the environment.

Perception

The author is very fond of telling audiences that there is 'no such thing as reality – there is only perception.' Although this might well raise a wry smile from the reader, I happen to believe that it is an incontrovertible truth. Everyone understands the world around them in a different manner – largely due to factors such as culture, education and upbringing. We are all the sum products of our experiences. We are all different and unique. Remember that stress and its onset is a personal thing – it is a *'perceived inability to cope'*. This therefore indicates that although the individual feels that they cannot cope, this may not in fact be true. However, to overcome this perception is a difficult thing – largely because people don't like to admit that they cannot or are not coping (consider culture once again), and so tend to remain silent and try their best to 'muddle through', all the time fearing that they are going to be 'found out' or derided in some manner by their peers or dismissed from their job (again consider uncertainty, workload and communication factors). The author would suggest that a PM who wishes to optimise both their team performance and the project delivery should attempt a **'Perception Alignment Strategy'**★ – providing a forum (based on this model) as a preventative/awareness methodology. In my opinion this is how high- performance project teams are created and excel.

Silver bullet: Stress is the direct progenitor of conflict within the project team environment. To combat stress and its onset, it is important to understand the causal factors that contribute directly to its manifestation. These factors are all inextricably linked and will vary in impact depending upon the particular case and the psychological make-up of the individuals involved. They are not, in every case, to be considered as having a strictly negative connotation – in some instances they might be an ameliorating factor.

STAKEHOLDER MANAGEMENT

As I mentioned above, the essence of project management is very simple: it's about people. BUT we must not focus solely on the project team. There are many other different individuals whom we must manage properly if we are to be a professional project manager and ensure the successful delivery of our project to the customer. Commonly, these 'other people' tend to be referred to as 'stakeholders' and the process of ensuring their (the stakeholders') happiness is generally known and accepted by the nomenclature of 'stakeholder management.' The author would even go so far as to state that he believes that not only will effective and efficient management of stakeholders ensure a successful project delivery but that this activity is essential and critical. A project operates at the best of times within an uncertain environment, and if there's one thing that is an absolute certainty, it does not operate in a vacuum!

The model shown in Figure 4.2 should be viewed as posing a number of basic questions (i.e. who the stakeholders are; where they are, and their position relative to our project). It is important to remember that not all stakeholders are of equal importance to the project; some may not have even heard of it or be aware of its (the project's) existence. To the uninitiated this might sound like a stupid statement — I assure you that it isn't. As we all know, any project progresses through a lifecycle (discussed earlier) and during this lifecycle different things happen — different activities may begin, in different locations, and there is (generally speaking) an increased level of resource consumption as the project moves into its actual execution phase. What this means is that as surely as the external environment continues to change, so too does the stakeholder mix. A classic example of stakeholders 'not existing' for an ongoing project — then 'existing' and becoming very powerful — is that of environmentalist

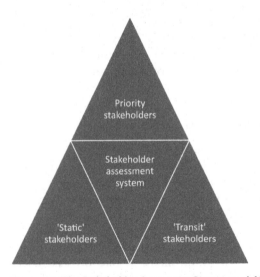

Figure 4.2 The Stakeholder Assessment System model*

groups. Many is the project that has unexpectedly (though these groups are now watched very carefully due to the importance placed on environmental issues and impacts) fallen foul of these stakeholders, with dire consequences.

The model takes a unique approach to stakeholder management – thinking about it from a different perspective. The 'top' triangle is where powerful and/or priority stakeholders are placed. The author utilises an inverted triangle to represent the concept that the organisation's (or project's) 'stakeholder assessment system' (note: not 'management' – the intention of this model is to be the precursor that shapes management strategy but remains a 'live' tool) is a 'dagger' that must delve deeply into the assessment of both 'static' and 'transit' stakeholders. The base of the inverted triangle therefore establishes a baseline as to who the current powerful and priority stakeholders are. 'Static' stakeholders in the model are those that it seems will be least likely to change or be affected by the project, while 'transit' stakeholders are those that may move either upward and become priority or sideways and become static. This part of the assessment system is where 'new' stakeholders will initially be classified prior to making a judgement as to the particular course of management required. The model must remain 'live' and be assessed with a frequency that is reflective of the volatility of the environment within which the project operates.

The Stakeholder Assessment System model will then allow the central crux to the problem of stakeholder management to be evaluated (i.e. the fact that different stakeholders all have their own agenda that they want to promote), leading to the classic situation of trying to keep everyone happy simultaneously, but knowing that this is an unrealistic expectation and is unlikely to be a winning strategy.

Silver bullet: Identify, assess, rank, prioritise, then – critically on the basis of these steps – CREATE RELATIONSHIPS that are SUSTAINABLE with as many of the stakeholders as you can. Believe me: the power in this (and the results that it generates) is almost incalculable. The author has been in more than one extremely 'sticky' situation and the day has been saved due to strong and positive relationships with other parties.

The importance of stakeholder management can never be overlooked or understated and has a direct correlation with one of today's burning questions of great strategic import – that of the acquisition and/or achievement of a competitive advantage. As I mentioned at the very beginning of this book, projects are increasingly utilised to allow organisations to attempt forays into the unknown – the very essence of what a project is allows control and defined resources. This therefore limits risk exposure to within these constrained allocations. Corporate activity exists to achieve a wide range of things – depending upon the organisation's mission and values – but all corporate entities wish to enjoy an advantage competitively over others in the same market. The fundamental problem underpinning the concept of 'competitive advantage' is that if you do achieve it, for example, by becoming the recognised market leader, or having the majority of the market share, or control of distribution channels, the reality is that any such advantage is going to be fleeting. In the last paragraph talking directly about stakeholder management (above), I strongly advocated the necessity of relationship creation. The reader may recall that I also made the point about how stakeholders could be both 'static' (i.e. unlikely to be interested in or affected by a project) or 'transit' – how they could change in their relative importance and how they could either cease to exist relative to a project, or be replaced with newer ones. This is an important point for the reader to grasp, as in this way stakeholder behaviour is mirrored directly by the concept of competitive advantage. What do I mean? Let us examine a number of parallels. Customers are definitely an important stakeholder group – having a visible presence in your chosen market, being known for quality/innovation/technology, etc. means that these customers are likely to purchase your products or do business with your organisation. But consumer (customer) tastes and interests change, and in response to this change in market conditions the organisation will have to consider its products or services against this change in demand. If it doesn't, then it is almost a forgone conclusion that any competitive advantage enjoyed by the organisation will cease to exist.

In recent years, organisations have come to realise that 'organisational knowledge' (i.e. the abilities that the organisation possesses through its employees and their experience) is a key component to the concept of a sustainable competitive advantage. We might seek a parallel here: within the domain of operating and delivering large, complex projects, experience and knowledge count for an inestimable amount. The author would even go so far as to postulate that this 'knowledge and experience' defines successful stakeholder management which, ultimately, leads to project success. The downside, of course, is the fact that both knowledge and particularly experiential-based knowledge takes time to acquire. I draw the reader's attention back to the point about capturing and utilising 'lessons learnt' documentation from previous projects. This cyclical process is captured in Figure 4.3.

It is an old adage that experience is gained over time and that there is no real substitute for this; hence the seeming dichotomy of the individual who gets the university degree but whose knowledge is not always on point, since it is not underpinned by practical experience. The only shortcut, really, is to have a great PM who will share and disseminate their knowledge gained by experience – though I would still suggest that we all need to 'experience' in order to learn (if we're smart).

The Time Cycle model (Figure 4.3) shows the process as to how organisational knowledge is created and hopefully captured (if it isn't

Figure 4.3 Acquiring organisational knowledge: the Time Cycle model

then it doesn't become organisational knowledge). As time passes and we learn about things, this enables us (as both organisations and individuals) to gain experience as we see how processes work and what the result is of things done or left undone. When we utilise experience and learning in order to do something, then we are applying knowledge. This knowledge can be further 'refined' if there is a lessons learnt process – a dissection if you will of what happened, what was good (we can reuse it next time), what was bad (we can avoid it next time) and what was new (emergent opportunities – different ways of doing things). This then gives us new organisational knowledge and when 'captured' and integrated (so as to be available to organisational members), then the organisation should evolve and may well gain some form of competitive advantage. This process should be perpetual.

5

PROJECT COMPONENTS

In this chapter, we will examine several of the key areas or 'components' to a project. Remember that, earlier on, we defined a project as something which had a series of activities to perform that would eventually result in the delivery of something – which was the purpose of the project's existence. In order to achieve this deliverable, the author would suggest that it is helpful to people if they understand how the various key processes come to be achieved within the lifespan of a project.

The first 'project component' the author would like to discuss is the project business case (PBC). This is the very important documentation that describes why a particular project exists. In order to achieve this, we may think of a PBC as being composed of two critical elements: the rationale for a project and the justification for the rationale. Let us examine these elements in turn. The rationale for a project contained within the PBC may be thought of as the 'high level' – the 'why' of the project. It is the 'fundamental reasoning' as to why this project exists (i.e. the 'overarching purpose' of the project). For example, the statement 'The construction of this ring road will enhance the local infrastructure and alleviate all traffic congestion problems' might represent the rationale for a project to build a ring road around a city with an underdeveloped or bad road infrastructure. The rationale informs the reader immediately as to the 'what' and the fundamental 'why' of the project. It is important that the reader understands that the project business case is the document that is most often the mechanism by which approval is granted for a project to go ahead and to receive funding (budget) from senior management or senior decision makers within the organisation. The

PBC is often used as a 'strategic chip' in the continual game of 'organisational poker.' If funding and approval are being sought, then typically the rationale for the existence and execution of a project will be aligned to the organisation's strategic focus (i.e. 'Hey everyone – here's how we can achieve what you want').

The second component of the PBC is the supporting arguments – the justifications. Consider the above-mentioned statement, 'The construction of this ring road will enhance the local infrastructure and alleviate all traffic congestion problems.' If this was the 'hook line' being used to convince decision makers, it might be further supported by justifications as to why the project should go ahead, why it makes sense. So, the justifications for our ring road project could be such things as:

> The cost to local industry due to choke points resultant from the necessity of having to navigate the city centre in order to reach the outlying suburbs and industrial estates is such that many smaller businesses have left the area. The ring road will entirely remove this problem by allowing traffic an easier, less congested and quicker time to destination. This is likely to act as an incentive to attract and sustain businesses within the city.

> As congestion will be relieved, this will lead to a positive impact on the level of emissions – particularly within the rush hour periods which currently experience slow movement due to present road infrastructure.

> The ring road will address a number of other issues such as complaints by local residents in the most congested areas of the city relative to noise (car horns) and [see point above] exhaust emissions.

> The modernisation of our road infrastructure will prolong existing infrastructure considerably due to the alleviation of wear and tear brought about by heavy traffic, thereby reducing our road maintenance and repair costs.

What the author hopes the reader 'sees' here is how powerful the PBC can be – it 'sells' the idea of the project by drawing attention to the myriad benefits to be realised and that there are many ways to achieve this, as demonstrated in the simple example above.

Silver bullet: Ensure that the justifications for your project encapsulate a spectrum of values and benefits – tailor them as best you can to ensure that they 'hit' a number of targets.

As you can see in the example above, I mention industry, social costs, environmental issues and cost savings – who could refuse?

It is a necessity that when you are going to present a PBC you have identified and categorised not only the tangible benefits (some or most of which may be obvious to the majority of the stakeholders) but also the intangible benefits which might, in fact, be more important – consider, for instance, the emphasis placed on 'local content.'

To step away from specifics for a moment, the author would encourage the reader to keep an open mind in terms of what is required for a particular PBC and what may be 'over-engineering' or 'surplus to requirements.'

Silver bullet: If you want to make your life easier and increase the chances of your project being accepted, get senior management support right from the beginning.

The more senior, the better for both of the above-mentioned parameters. Beware though: it is quite often easy to illicit support from a 'senior manager' as long as it isn't going to actually ever bother them – a completely different kettle of fish if you want their support and actual involvement. The author can tell you from many an experience that the idea conceptually or in principle is fine with senior figures – as long as it doesn't interfere with their day. So you will need to be very sure of who you are going to approach to be your 'project sponsor' – they are after all going to be your 'champion' and if they don't really want to be involved I would strongly urge the reader to look elsewhere.

A friend of mine once classified his job as a PM as being 'the filter' that protects the project team from s...t from above and allows his project to continue with its execution and delivery unmolested. I would suggest to you that a good 'project sponsor' is a higher level filter that should do the same for you. It is also worth pointing out to the reader that there is no de-facto methodology for PBCs – no 'universally accepted template.' They may well be prescribed by organisational processes, but there are no 'rules' stating that a PBC could be created or altered/amended informally if that was permitted within an organisation. The author would advocate careful consideration of all the factors discussed thus far pertaining to PBCs and treat them all on a case-by-case basis rather than making assumptions and merely applying the 'organisational template' (if one exists).

The list below is, in the author's opinion, a comprehensive one in terms of what should be included within a project business case. I am by no means attempting to suggest that this list is exhaustive or that it should be followed to the letter; rather it is my intention to offer the list as a helpful guide to the reader should they find themselves uncertain as to what to include in a PBC or are simply looking for some new ideas or ways of approaching the creation or formulation of one. The list is not 'ranked' in any order of importance.

'Inclusive elements' of a project business case are as follows:

- Overview/executive summary
- Statement of scope
- Statement of resources
- Time/cost estimates
- Risk analysis
- Stakeholder analysis
- Project deliverables
- KPIs (key performance indicators) and CSFs (critical success factors)
- Ownership/responsibility and reporting architecture

The author would like to make a specific comment about KPIs and CSFs in the list above. I am certain that everyone involved in projects possesses absolute clarity as to what is meant by a KPI – for example, a 'stage gate' or a 'milestone' being reached during the lifecycle of a project. However, the author frequently encounters individuals who think that the terms 'KPI' and 'CSF' are interchangeable: this is a bad mistake to make.

KPIs are a point of reference within the lifespan of a project that is indicative of a measure of progress towards project completion. Two of the most common forms are mentioned above. KPIs are important for a number of reasons – contracts often have sums payable at certain 'points of achievement' within the lifespan of the project. Resource requirements can be reassessed in line with current project status. Stakeholder management should be revisited at these points, to name a few.

Critical success factors (CSFs) should be differentiated from KPIs, since they are more important. Should they be incorrectly handled, it is likely that the project will fail. Examples of CSFs might be an 'event horizon,' the lead time of a critical component, or even something natural such as the weather impacting on infrastructure (rain/temperature) and operations. In short, CSFs should always be identified at the initiation phase of a project and it is helpful to categorise them separately (yet not necessarily mutually exclusively) from KPIs as things that will cause the project to fail if they do not occur

What all this means therefore is that the PBC will become increasingly important as the vehicle that ensures that the project scope is 'tight and right' (discussed below) and that all relevant issues (such as those discussed above) are addressed and given the requisite attention to feed directly into the planning phase.

The next 'project component' the author would like to highlight is that of the project sponsor. Project sponsors are very important – period. If one considers the reality of resource constraints from both the organisational perspective and the project perspective, then (particularly within larger organisations which may be running programmes or portfolios of many projects) it is likely that any given project will face significant competition internally from other projects requiring funding and resourcing. This brings us back to the individual mentioned earlier, namely the project sponsor. The reader will remember that a little earlier the author recounted a story about how a friend who was a project manager regarded his job as a 'filter' to protect the project team from things directly outside the project delivery. Perhaps the reader should consider the concept of the project sponsor as 'a higher level filter,' being able to operate at a more senior level than the PM, acting as the 'champion' of the project, and protecting it (and the PM + team) from 'higher level' issues (to be politically correct). So the project sponsor should be thought of as the interface or linkage between the corporate (strategic) and tactical (operational) levels of the organisation.

Silver bullet: Whoever a 'project sponsor' happens to be, they should possess both power and influence within the organisation (i.e. they will have authority and can act as a change agent).

The reality is that this is another dimension of organisational politics. Given the statements made above regarding resource constraints and the probability of internal competition, then the project with the most senior (and therefore most powerful) project sponsor is the project in the best position. So, one of the key attributes that is desirable within a project sponsor is an individual with a good dose of political acumen, one who has been around and knows the ropes and knows how to get things done within the organisational system.

It is worth pointing out to the reader that the appointment of a project sponsor need not be some kind of formal procedure – a project sponsor could easily be appointed through some informal mechanism (i.e. due to some form of relationship). It is important, though, that however a project sponsor comes to be appointed, they will remain with the project – thereby providing continuity. The author has seen project sponsors change multiple times on larger projects and has noticed the detrimental effect this can have.

Silver bullet: Keep the same project sponsor (wherever possible) through the lifecycle of the project.

Silver bullet: Don't acquire a project sponsor in name only.

The author has seen many a senior manager, when asked if they would be a project sponsor, agree, then state that 'they don't want ever to be bothered by anything to do with the project in question, but are happy to lend their name.' No good at all, folks. Also, if a project dictates (it might be a joint venture or some other form of collaborative undertaking) that there is a requirement for multiple individuals to fulfil the role of 'project sponsors,' *never* have an even number – this is death for decision making. In this situation, the author would suggest the establishment of a 'project board'. This is a formal mechanism consisting of at least three senior individuals tasked with undertaking the sponsorship role (the author would suggest that three is probably the optimum amount of people to have). Some readers might be more familiar with this concept as a 'project steering committee' (same thing, more or less).

One point to reiterate: the project sponsor is not a part of the project team; rather, they should be considered as an 'external resource' or ally to the project (consider the use of the term 'champion' stated earlier).

The next 'project component' is perhaps the most important of them all – the project scope. The author would suggest to the reader that if you knew next to nothing about project management and were to walk around taking a 'straw poll' at a conference of project management professionals, the most common answer to the question of why projects were late, over budget or just simply failures, the two words 'project scope' would feature in the majority of replies you received. So what, exactly, is a project scope? Well, the simplest way to picture it is that it (very much like a microscope' or a 'periscope) provides a specific focus on certain things. Consider the mention above of some other types of 'scope' – the analogy is sound; a scope captures what it is looking at – it is not interested (per se) in anything outside of its focus. This is the essence of the project scope – it identifies what is to be included within a project (i.e. what its (the project's) deliverables are) and, by this token, it ignores the 'exclusions' (i.e. things that are not 'captured within the focus' of the scope – things that will not be subject to the project execution, nor covered by the project's budget).

This is a straightforward process, yet the issues around 'scoping' are myriad and convoluted and are often the central crux as to why a project encounters difficulties later during its life when it is discovered that something crucial has been omitted from the budgetary calculations, or that the scope was made too wide; subsequently, delivery is going to be problematic to say the least.

There is a further dimension to this issue which goes by the name of 'scope creep.' Scope creep exists due to a variety of reasons, the most common being that a client decides to alter the scope of the project's deliverables somehow. Generally, changes such as those that fall under the 'scope creep domain' are considered to be small 'tweaks' here and there – perhaps an additional quantity of something, or a different colour, or perhaps a slight specification change.

The author would draw the reader's attention to a point here. For whatever strange foible in the minds of people, individuals seem to be fixated on the idea that a change to the scope implies more work. This is, of course, completely true – but does not necessitate that the change is always larger. The client may have decided that they wish to make a reduction in the scope – perhaps a reduction in numbers of items, or perhaps a change of quality specifications (i.e. not wanting to 'over-engineer' something, or a cheaper financial cost).

The danger of scope creep is twofold. First, these small deviations/modifications of the project scope tend to multiply and culminate in some kind of 'critical mass,' where the project manager and/or project team realise that the amount of these small changes has now placed the current project progress quite significantly away from the original schedule. The implications of this are, of course, time and money. Second, scope creep should be considered to be inexorably tied with project change orders. If a client wishes to alter the scope of the project for any reason whatsoever, it is both sensible and prudent for a change order to be raised documenting the required change. This establishes an audit trail and could become important in the event that something goes wrong, or if there is insufficient budget left for completion due to these changes (hopefully any change in cost is detailed and agreed within the change order).

Silver bullet: From a project control perspective, it is easier (in terms of both time and money) to correct a minor deviation from the scope than to attempt to deal with a major variation at some future point – not to mention the raft of potential implications such as breach of contract, delay, EOT (extension of time) arguments (particularly within the domain of EPC projects), arbitration or even litigation.

The author has had many friends who, when managing projects, are asked to make changes by the client, and nearly all of them have expressed the view (to the author) that they find it uncomfortable to enter into this process of formal documentation for what is, after all, a small change with a client or client representative for fear of causing offence or damaging the relationship. My response would be that if you have a good relationship with a client or their representative then this shouldn't be a problem, as it provides protection for all parties who might be involved with any such change.

Silver bullet: Never, ever, make any change to an agreed project scope without a signed change order providing both the authorisation and the specification/quantification of any requested change, including any time and cost implications.

The reader should consider a direct parallel between the project scope and the need to deal with scope creep. The scope documentation for the project as a whole should be considered as a 'formalising process,' as it exists to define what the project is going to deliver and what it is not. Likewise, change orders specifying or documenting alterations and changes to the project scope should always be considered to be a formalising process, as it is documenting the 'new' or 'updated' project scope which will therefore impact upon both schedule and resource requirements.

PROJECT INTERFACE MANAGEMENT

If the essence of project management is about the leadership and coordination of a team of specialist people and other stakeholders, then surely it must also be fundamentally about the management of interfaces. An interface is, in the author's opinion, that 'area' or 'zone' where different parties interact with one another. This can impact both negatively (competition/disputes) or positively (cooperation). In project management parlance an interface is the 'transitional zone' where stakeholders meet. This could be internally (e.g. finance and engineering) or externally (e.g. engineering and outsourced fabricator/subcontractor). The simplest way to convey the idea of what an interface is is to consider a simple Venn type diagram such as the one shown in Figure 6.1.

Silver bullet: The efficient management of interfaces is a critical success factor for a project's delivery – it should be monitored and controlled very carefully.

Establishing who is going to be in control of what and to whom they are going to report is surely nothing other than simple common sense and the application of logic towards designing an architecture that will enable the interfaces between all involved stakeholders to have clarity and visibility as to who is doing what. The author would strongly urge the reader at the project initiation stage (or earlier) to simply sit down and think this through – thereby creating the mechanism(s) required for effective control (consider points made regarding scope creep).

DOI: 10.4324/9781003188964-7

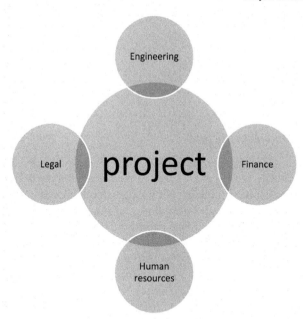

Figure 6.1 Functional interfaces with a project

It is important to remember that the issues discussed above are of increasing relevance the bigger a project is. There are three critical factors that have a directly proportional relationship to the project and its delivery as a 'project' grows in size. The bigger the project, the more complex it will be. Complexity equates to difficulties in control as there will be more interfaces requiring active management, more stakeholders, and more procurement and lead time management issues – so therefore more cost implications (a bigger budget), etc.

The author believes that the importance of project interface management should never be overlooked and that the process of effectively managing these interfaces consists of a number of key factors that should be closely examined throughout the life of any project. These are as follows:

1   Organisational/project structure
2   Project control system

3 Communication and information flow
4 Technology
5 Cooperation
6 Competition
7 Political behaviour
8 Self-organisation

Organisational/project structure

Projects in themselves are often utilised as the vehicles with which organisations are able to 'test the waters' of new ideas, products or markets. The 'project methodology' allows a greater degree of control due to the concept of triple constraints (i.e. time, cost, budget) and therefore also serves to limit risk exposure (not writing 'blank cheques'). This said, there is still a wide range of both project capability and success that differs across organisations. The author would postulate that how the organisation itself is configured (and therefore how it tends to configure projects) is in itself a critical success factor across the delivery interface within the triple constraints mentioned above. The organisational configuration or structure will also be a by-product of the organisational culture. The author would highlight to the reader here that this (the culture aspect) underpins most of the discussion within the factors to follow. It is important to understand that every organisation has a culture that is unique unto itself and that this reflects the how and why of how the organisation behaves both in general and across different interfaces – be they either internal or external to the organisation.

The project control system

My father was a military man – his whole life was spent in the Navy. He was very fond of saying that 'the problem with common sense is that it isn't very common.' When I look across projects and project delivery, it appears that this particular expression couldn't be truer. Over-engineering, miscommunication, political behaviour (discussed below) or simple folly are some of the main ingredients in the recipe for disaster – and most of them could easily be avoided in my opinion. There is an underlying dynamic that should be borne in mind relative to 'how' a particular project is controlled. The larger and therefore more complex the project the more difficult it becomes to manage or control, as there tends to be an exponential growth in the number of interfaces that must be managed. Thus the project control system should, in the first instance, be scalable in order to deal with progressive levels of magnitude and complexity. Every project is unique, but the author would suggest that there are common aspects that, if managed properly, serve to enable successful interface management within the project team. The 'big three' to me are as follows:

1   Ownership
2   Accountability
3   Reporting structures

In the author's experience as a consultant, it continues to surprise me how these three relatively obvious, simple aspects seem to go haywire at some point during the project's lifecycle (most notably – but not exclusively by any means – within the execution phase). There is often confusion within the project team as to who is a task or work package owner – what they are accountable for and who reports to them and who they in turn report to. These protocols are not difficult to establish but continue to be one of those enduring foibles of project management that often become the root cause of project delay, rework, resource wastage, or – even worse – project failure. The author would suggest that early attention paid to these interfaces will reap long-lasting benefits both to the project from a delivery perspective as well as to the project team members themselves – by having a more defined environment and clarity in work that needs to be done. This should form the basis as well as the central aspect of the project stakeholder management plan.

Communication and information flow

The author is of the opinion that there are two things generally wrong with people: they don't listen and they don't communicate, or, to be fairer, they don't do either of the aforementioned well. As a project is a team endeavour, I would suggest that this is far from ideal – a team's function (and therefore performance) is directly impacted by the extent to which information and communication is shared throughout the project architecture. Obviously, information should be shared on a 'need to know' basis, as not everything is for the eyes and ears of everyone – often confidentiality is critical, particularly if the project is R&D/cutting edge and involves strategic implications such as new product development or new process technology. This aside, the sharing of information and effective communication are two critical factors that need planning and attention in terms of dissemination, confidentiality and project control monitoring/reporting protocols.

Silver bullet: Time is never wasted when investing it in developing strong, positive and mutually beneficial relationships – place emphasis on effective communication and management of information and its flow.

Technology

From the interface management perspective, technology is often a key enabler. If the reader considers the discussion thus far in this chapter, then it becomes obvious that technology itself provides a forum for communication and enhances (and depends upon) information in order to support organisational/project function.

Many projects are themselves enabled through the advent of ever-increasing software capabilities (e.g. 'IT' projects, military technologies, R&D, to name a few), but as technology continues to develop and accelerate, consider how it has made the 'geographically dispersed' project team a reality – direct verbal communication, the exchange of documents and information, often in (almost) real time. Of course, while technology is itself a great enabler for interface management, it also brings a new level of complexity through the creation of multiple new interfaces such as the human/computer interface. How many times have you struggled to complete a simple or mundane task due to a system failure – or simply due to unfamiliarity with the 'how' to do things? I am very fond of saying that 'technology is great, as long as it works.' It is undoubtable, even inevitable, that the role and influence of technology will continue to both create and drive new and existing interfaces. The author would suggest that as a direct result of this, the successful management of interfaces both within projects and the world at large will be the source of sustainable competitive advantage to the organisations that 'get it right.'

The author would suggest that the reader might consider this issue from the following perspective: 'As technology gives to some, so it takes from others.' What do I mean? Consider the nature of competition – everyone competing wishes to maximise their gain (be it monetary, market share, brand recognition, etc.), and the path to this is often through uniqueness, what is popularly termed the 'USP', the unique selling point. The USP of an organisation might be proprietary technology in itself; it could be access to and/ or control of distribution channels; it could be quality; it could be speed – the list is pretty long. However, if we think of the kinds of things listed above, it should be apparent to the reader how technology plays a direct role in everything mentioned. As I stated at the start of this paragraph, technology increasingly provides the 'key' with which to optimise the interface – it can create the interface; it can manage the interface, or it can do both. Food for thought.

COMPETITION AND COOPERATION

I would like to share another hypothesis with you. As mentioned at the start of this chapter, there are only, broadly speaking, two kinds of interface – period: those that are competitive and those that are cooperative. If we stop to consider this rather bold statement and we cast our mental eye over what we know about interfaces and their management, there are no interfaces regardless of who or what is involved that are not captured by this statement. Let us illuminate this point by considering a few examples:

1 Two organisations have complementary proprietary technology. They consider forming a joint venture in order to strengthen or consolidate their share of a particular market while simultaneously creating an enhanced mutual protection from competition from others. This is a cooperative interface.
2 An organisation with the latest cutting-edge technology is able to redefine a production process within its industry and market and derives cost efficiencies that cannot be matched. This is a competitive interface.

3   A project manager secures additional finance for a project team due to the strength of their (the PM's) positive informal relationships with key organisational stakeholders. This is a cooperative interface.

4   A large company executes a successful hostile takeover of a smaller company that consolidates its market leadership position. This is a competitive interface.

An interesting point about the above examples is that they might be viewed from the opposite perspective. This is an important aspect of interface management – the perspective of any particular stakeholder relative to the interface. There is a complex relationship between competition and cooperation. Certainly, while they may represent two sides of a metaphorical 'coin' they also mirror each other by their very existence. Consider: due to competition, some organisations cooperate (example 1), but to the market and other competitors this is a competitive gambit on behalf of the organisations in question. In example 3 the PM is able to leverage relationships they have informally, so while this is most definitely cooperation in action ('friends' helping) this could be at the detriment of other projects and PMs within the organisation as they miss out due to resource constraints. So they (other projects or PMs) would view this action as being deliberately competitive.

Silver bullet: Whether or not an interface is viewed as being competitive or cooperative in nature is totally dependent upon the perspective of a particular stakeholder or stakeholder grouping relative to the interface in question.

Political behaviour

So now, perhaps, we arrive at the heart of the problem – political behaviour. I am not referring to those individuals allegedly engaged in activities for the benefit of us all, but rather to how people behave within their organisations. Humans are curious creatures and are not always either logical or rational in what they do and how they do it. I would go so far as to say that political behaviour which is partisan and negative is like a cancer that will ultimately destroy the organisation, and unfortunately it's endemic. Political behaviour is about self-interest; empire building and the acquisition/deployment of power. In a world of corporate political correctness, the undercurrents of manipulation and exploitation run deeply throughout the veins of organisational cultures. Regrettably, projects (often competing internally for limited resources) are sometimes caught in the political crossfire. At the risk of sounding both cynical and jaded, when walking into an organisation for the first time and seeing the 'vision' and 'mission' statements prominently adorning the walls of the reception area, proudly announcing to all comers its core values and beliefs, the embodiment of the organisation's culture, it often brings a fleeting wry smile (after all, we must remain professional), quickly replaced by suitable gravitas. Why? You may ask. Well, simply because I wonder just exactly how many employees of the company adhere to them, know of their existence or, to be frank, even care.

The essence of the problem is, in my opinion, self-interest. Some of us simply desire to get ahead of our colleagues and are not particularly concerned as to the methodology employed. Some organisational cultures with which the author is familiar actually encourage this type of 'latent aggression': push forward, work hard, be in first, leave last, be at your desk on weekends ... oh look, there's someone who is not a team player leaving at a normal time to go home and see their spouse and children. I'm sure most of you reading this have been there.

Earlier on I mentioned power. It is very important to understand that power is distributed throughout an organisation in two parallel, simultaneous ways – formally and informally. Formal power may stem from seniority and/or job title/role within the organisation, while informal power tends to be reflected via relationships (i.e. common interests and activities). The old adage 'the road to hell is paved with good intentions' carries a lot of weight within the context discussed here. To be less jaded and cynical for a moment: I have no doubt that there are many people out there trying to make a better organisation with a better culture – ultimately the true value of any company is represented by its people and their talents, skills and abilities. Those who like to play political games for their own ends should think about this and stop trying to undermine positive, value-adding processes and activities.

From the project management perspective, I would make two suggestions. First, don't partake in political behaviour – it's destructive, petty and may well backfire on you. Second, don't tolerate these sorts of people within your project team – they are corrosive and counterproductive and can cause great harm. Be very clear with the team on this matter: we're a team, we look out for each other, we work together to deliver our project. Whenever I have found any of these sorts of individuals in my project teams I have immediately rooted them out – complete zero tolerance is my mantra here.

Silver bullet: Project success is wholly dependent upon the collaborative and collective endeavours of the team. Politically driven individuals do not have the team's interests at heart – they have their own. Do not, under any circumstance, tolerate these types of people in your project team; they are anathema to success.

SELF-ORGANISATION

This is often confused with ideas such as empowerment – but it is completely different. Self-organisation (hereafter SO) is found throughout the world – it exists in physics and it exists in nature. SO is directly applicable to complex adaptive corporate systems and to projects due to their very inherent nature. SO is the emergence of a 'sudden' new behaviour which is so beneficial to the entire system that the entire system adapts itself to harness the benefit. All the key elements discussed in this chapter are the components of this process. This idea is explored and explained in greater detail in another upcoming book in the series, *The Silver Bullets of Self-organisation: Managing Adaptive Complex Interfaces.*

In closing this particular discussion, I leave you, the reader, with a last thought on interfaces – taking everything said in this chapter, please remember the following 'silver bullet':

Silver bullet: Interactions between people of different cultures is probably the key interface to be managed – many projects are international in nature and there is often a 'cross-pollination/interaction' which involves the exchange

of values, beliefs and cultural norms throughout the value chain. Another critically important aspect of this interface is that of time – time that is lost is lost and we cannot have it back. So, time lost through misunderstandings, miscommunications or lack of cultural awareness/sensitivity has potentially huge ramifications if mishandled.

PROJECT BUDGETARY MANAGEMENT

We have established that projects often operate in terms of imposed constraints – generally encapsulated by time and cost. This may be reflected in non-availability of materials or expertise (hence delay through 'waiting'), or it may manifest in terms of a price escalation in something critical such as a key raw material and there is insufficient budget to cover this change. So, there are two sub-components to this: the need to be good at 'trade-off' decision making and being prepared (to whatever degree is possible) to have anticipated the change and its impacts ahead of it happening (i.e. robust risk management) – thereby having contingency funds available. But this is not as easy as it sounds – particularly the second point just made. One of the truly unfathomable mysteries of the corporate world to me has always been the reaction of the finance department when 'negotiating' over contingency allocations in project budgets/funds. The author has explained numerous times to various financial people that the contingency money is there to deal with changes to the environment and that if we don't need it we won't use it. It is at this point that you realise they are looking at you like you have just asked them to provide the funds from their own personal bank accounts! This mystery also has another rather interesting codicil – if you save money and deliver a project under budget then your budget the following year/project will be cut by the amount you just saved. Need I say anymore?

There has to be a realisation, when considering resources, that cash is not only 'still king' but should be considered as the 'cornerstone' resource. Why? Because it is the resource that allows you to acquire all other resources.

DOI: 10.4324/9781003188964-8

The budgetary process: below, I list the steps I take in order when attempting to get budgetary approval (aka 'funding') for a project. You may consider using this as a template if you so wish. Many of the steps below have already been discussed, but I would like to comment further on steps 5 and 7 specifically.

1   Establishment of project scope
2   Projected costs
3   Risk analyses
4   Formal creation
5   Approval
6   Monitoring/control/reporting protocols
7   Budget becomes 'live'

It is important to remember that prior to approval a budget doesn't actually exist, so to quote the vernacular in point (7) above, it does not become 'live.' In relation to point (5) above, bear in mind the earlier discussion on the distribution of power throughout the organisation (both formal and informal) and regrettably, organisational politics. Both will be very pertinent in the budgetary approval process – even if people would be disinclined to comment (an answer in itself) or deny that this is so. I would imagine those of you reading this book with some experience of these issues are probably smiling and nodding your heads at this point. Let us examine some of the other contributory factors in terms of 'budgetary problems.'

First, it goes right back to that old thing called 'communication.' Another enduring corporate mystery to me is the ever-present lack of people within a project/organisational structure who should be informed – yet for reasons unknown are not – (and I mean key decision makers), resulting in the typical non-progression, uncertainty and confusion as to what is happening, when and how. Time goes by, nothing happens. Sometimes, again for a plethora of possible reasons, budgetary amounts seem to be completely misaligned with the scope and project business case documentation (i.e. woefully inadequate). The contingency discussion aside, it seems that often budgetary allocations seem to have been assigned in an almost arbitrary manner. Does this occur due to misinformed/uniformed management and decision makers? Is it due to faulty/bad information? Have ridiculous risk assumptions been made? Or is it because of deliberate ignorance or lack of interest in lessons learnt from previous projects? I leave you, the reader, to be the judge and jury of this one – though, for what it's worth, I would suspect that many if not all of the questions above are part of the problem – perhaps singularly, perhaps collectively.

Silver bullet: The ultimate purpose of a budget is to efficiently procure, allocate and utilise resources.

Some further 'silver bullets':

1 **Ensure who needs to be involved is involved**
2 **Budgeting is a critical component of the planning process – do it properly**
3 **Avoid making assumptions**

PROJECT SCHEDULING

The field of project management has a problem. It is a problem of our own making and one unlikely to be resolved anytime soon. This problem is the over-reliance on technology. I am referring to this from the perspective of project scheduling. While all the software packages available are both important and essential and enable project execution to occur, this is not the essence of the problem. The essence of the problem is ignorance – how many mistakes have caused rework/delay/ lack of funding due to a figure or value represented somewhere in a software graphic – where the erroneous information was placed there by human error? I would imagine a lot – a whole lot. The big problem with technology of this type is that it is only as good as the information it receives.

So, you may be beginning to wonder – why state the obvious? The reason why the author makes this statement is because of the number of individuals he has encountered who have been responsible for just such errors. These errors, though, have been made due to the fact that the individual in question is contributing to a process they don't understand. So, what exactly am I driving at? I'm talking about project scheduling. I'm not talking about inputting the data – I'm talking about understanding and knowing why you're inputting the data (i.e. what this information means to the project in the real world). This is an important point and one that should not be underestimated. What I am suggesting here is that if someone really understood what scheduling was all about then some information or behaviour of the schedule should sound a mental warning bell (e.g. 'this doesn't seem right' or 'this can't be correct … it will have a disastrous impact on X or Y'). They wouldn't simply accept the

DOI: 10.4324/9781003188964-9

information blindly; they might pause to think for a moment – check and investigate – and they may well have prevented a negative impact upon the project's delivery. As anyone involved in project management knows, the earlier an error or mistake is spotted the quicker it can be resolved with less cost and therefore impact. Below, I have listed some of the key aspects of project scheduling that I think serve to inject some clarity into the entire process of project scheduling:

- Scheduling is a critical project activity
- Enables effective deployment and consumption of designated resources
- Ensures the point above is where and when
- Provides a critical component of planning and execution of a project
- May serve as an 'early warning' of deviation
- Should inform performance measurement

One of the most critical aspects of scheduling to understand is that there is not necessarily a single way to do it – there could be multiple ways of structuring the schedule dependent upon a wide range of factors. The first that comes to mind is availability of a key resource – perhaps expertise or technology/equipment/plant. If something is not available within a desired time window, and it is that particular item/person which is needed, then obviously the schedule will have to be planned for/be capable of alteration in order to accommodate this.

Silver bullet: There are only two kinds of project activities – sequential and parallel.

This brings me to a central scheduling issue – the concept of precedence. It is important, perhaps even imperative, that the individual tasked with managing the schedule has absolute understanding of precedence. So, what do I mean when I speak of 'precedence' or 'precedential relationships'? Well, the major clue lies within the term 'preceding' (i.e. being a forerunner to something). Consider the silver bullet above – some project activities can only start when a 'preceding activity' is either finished or has reached a particular stage; other activities can begin simultaneously. What makes precedence critical to project scheduling was mentioned at the start of the earlier (or preceding!) paragraph. A particular schedule configuration may not be the only one and may not be the optimum one either. This brings us to the idea of 'criticality.' As I'm sure most readers engaged within project management would know, some activities regardless of whether they are sequential or parallel are 'critical' – hence the 'critical path' through a project's activities. A critical activity therefore lies upon the critical path in the schedule. It is an activity that has no 'slack' or 'float' time. What this means is that this particular activity has to be performed when it is scheduled to do so – it cannot be delayed or postponed. If it has to start on Monday and finish on Friday then this is what it must do.

The concept of 'float' or 'slack' is often represented in Gantt Charts as a portion of the activity in a different colour or left open (i.e. non-shaded). Gantt Charts (GCs) are fairly straightforward. The key features of a GC are that the critical path activities tend to run along the top of the chart. Activities are listed vertically down the left-hand side, while time tends to be the subject matter of the horizontal axis. Activities and their duration tend to be in the shape of boxes or 'bricks.' Obviously, the bigger the box and the more time/resources it will require will denote attention in the planning/scheduling (even if it is not a critical activity). Precedential relationships between activities tend to be represented by vertical lines linking them. To understand the very elemental key to scheduling, consider the example below.

Activity X

Duration three days
Float two days

This basic information leads to several important scheduling considerations:

1   What is the earliest start date?
2   What is the earliest finish date?
3   What is the latest start date?
4   What is the latest finish date?

All things being equal, we can see that it would be likely that Activity X will take place during a working week (i.e. Monday to Friday), but because it only has a duration of three days and a float of two, there is some flexibility as to when we could start and finish – and this flexibility might well be useful if there are resource constraints (such as something/someone being unavailable on a particular day).

So, the earliest day we could start would be Monday (day 1)

The earliest time that the activity would be competed (finish time) would be Wednesday (day 3)

We could start on Tuesday (day 2) and this would mean that we finished on Thursday (day 4)

The latest possible start time would be Wednesday (day 3), meaning that the latest possible completion (finish) would be Friday (day 5)

This very simple example contains the very essence of scheduling flexibility. If Activity X was a critical activity it might have to begin on Monday (day 1) and end on Wednesday (day 3) and would have zero float time.

So, to sum up the five main reasons why precedence is so important:

1 Identifies whether an activity is parallel or sequential
2 Aids in resource estimation
3 Identifies (or initiates) a different schedule layout/path
4 Very useful for 'staged' procurement strategies
5 Complements the demarcation of 'milestones'

THE WORK BREAKDOWN STRUCTURE

There is a directly proportional (yet inverse) relationship between complexity and control (i.e. the more 'complex' something is the harder it is to control properly – (greater number of stakeholders/ activities/interfaces, etc.). A true lifesaver for any project (but, in the author's view, especially large/complex ones) is the work breakdown structure (WBS). The WBS 'explodes' the project into all of its activities and sub-activities. This makes it very much a visual tool – with a lot of information available at a glance. WBS are, by and large, depicted as a hierarchy. So, the first box in the middle of the page will tend to have the project's name within it. As mentioned earlier, the activities and sub-activities are progressively broken down layer by layer (depicted by subsequent layers of boxes with their 'origin' linkage shown by vertical lines). A simple example is given in Figure 8.1.

The reader will note the use of the words 'work packages' (WPs). The author is personally a big fan of WPs. They bring a lot of benefits to a project. First, one should consider them almost as if they were a 'mini-project' in themselves. In industries such as the international oil and gas business, some work packages are bigger than other complete projects in terms of time, resources and budget in other industries. The WP also contains its own scope – what it is existing to do and what will be excluded from it; this is very useful for scheduling. A WP should also have a designated 'owner' (consider this individual as a 'sub-project manager' or, if you like, an assistant PM). As ownership is assigned, as well as time, resources and budget, it becomes easy for the overall PM (and team members) to understand reporting requirements/relationships, as well as accountability. In my experience, this goes a long way towards effective control and coordination and provides an excellent mechanism on which to formulate project monitoring protocols such as information 'flow' (dissemination) and task delegation. Remember, an informed team is a team that can do its job and deliver. So, in the very simplistic example given above, how many potential WPs are there? We must be careful here. The number of WPs is wholly

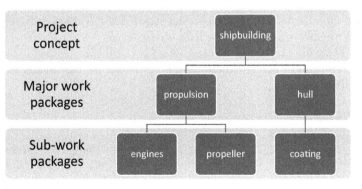

Figure 8.1 A simple WBS showing a project structure

dependent upon the particular project – its size, scope and complexity may dictate the number of given WPs. This number might also be at the behest of the PM or senior management – there is no universal formula as to what number of WPs there should be in the planning/execution of a project.

Silver bullet: A work package (WP) should be considered as a discreet 'chunk' of a project – so it is *de facto* a 'mini, or sub-project' in itself with designated resources and a defined owner.

If the author was in charge of the example given above, I would consider that there are two WPs contained within this WBS – one handling 'propulsion,' the other the hull. As stated, though, this is not a necessity – it is open to choice of the individual(s) who are the decision makers.

As in many things there is a potential for the WBS to become a negative force – to be made overcomplicated for no real reason/purpose, and, most importantly, to be misused as a tool for micro-management. Of all possible outcomes of a project as it is underway, the worst possible occurrence in the author's opinion is the manifestation of micro-management. When this happens, the chances of successful delivery within the iron triangle criteria of time, cost and quality diminish exponentially. Why? the reader may ask. The answer is relatively simple. Micro-management makes people feel that they are neither trusted nor competent and it makes people demotivated. I always see it in my mind as a simple relationship formula: MM = negative project performance. Take my advice: don't micro-manage – all you'll do is mismanage.

Silver bullet: Micro-management equates to the death of project success.

RESOURCE MANAGEMENT

All projects exist to do something, to deliver something. As we have established thus far, projects are human endeavours that utilise and consume resources over time towards a desired outcome. As the reader is also no doubt aware, the majority of projects rarely deliver within time and budget, or to the required quality. In this section, the Author hopes to show how having a clearer understanding of the 'resource dimension' of project management can enhance success.

The basic classifications of resources are as follows:

1 Land
2 Labour
3 Capital
4 Knowledge/skill/experience
5 Technology

When considering the nature of resources and what the ramifications are of availability, ownership and cost, the author would suggest that we examine this subject from the perspective of competition. As we have established thus far in this book, project management and the use of projects as the vehicle to enter into newer markets, to explore untested strategies and initiatives, to effect organisational change is fundamentally about the search for sustainable competitive advantage. No organisation can be competitive (or in fact achieve anything at all) without access to or ownership of resources. Indeed, these very types of corporate leverage are, the author would suggest, the fundamental dynamic which underpins commercial activity (and therefore competitive and cooperative ventures).

It is an old maxim that 'the true capital of any organisation is its people.' I agree wholeheartedly – but people and their knowledge, skills, talents and abilities are only a component of the corporate resource dynamic. An organisation might require land – for its offices, or for the very nature of its business (i.e. warehousing), or even more directly – it could be the central thing that the organisation 'does' (e.g. mining). The important distinction that must be made from both a project and a wider business sense regarding land is to understand that there are several key dimensions of consideration:

1 Ownership: Does the organisation own the land in question? Where is the land/property situated (consider the primacy of city centre locations for establishing a corporate image for the organisation/HQ)? How much land does the organisation own? Does this fulfil strategic/operational aspirations? If the

organisation doesn't own the land/buildings, etc. then it must rent. What are the costs of rental (likely to be location-dependent). What is the degree of infrastructure? What access/use of supporting infrastructure does the organisation possess/enjoy? Are there any limitations/regulations associated with the use/ownership of the land (i.e. environmental compliance – consider what this can cost if the organisation 'gets it wrong'). We must also consider potential project activities from a corporate social responsibility perspective – how is the organisation and its activities perceived by the relevant stakeholders? This can get very serious for the organisation and its image/reputation.

2   Labour: It is important to point out here that the term 'labour' encapsulates all levels of human input/skills/knowledge/abilities – it is not simply a reference to manual, unskilled labour. From the project perspective, labour is important for two main reasons. First, its availability, and second, its degree of competence. What I mean by the latter is the level of skill and expertise possessed by the labour force within any geographical domain. The author has seen instances of local content laws stipulating that 'X' amount of the workforce on a project must contain local people. The problem arises for the foreign contractor when the local 'engineers,' for example, are not to the necessary standard so as to perform engineering tasks and duties to the level required internationally in terms of safety and quality (as well as the cost/efficiency relationship). If a project is going to be operated in a foreign locale and is subject to local content provisions, one yardstick to assess competency issues would be to look at education demographics and the number of universities within that jurisdiction and to assess what types of degrees they offer and the reputation of the various programmes and their graduates.

Two further important classifications of resources that must be actively managed are as follows:

1   Capital: I often consider capital as the 'cornerstone' resource, since it is the resource that allows the organisation to procure other resources. The old adage 'cash is king' should possibly be altered to 'working capital management is king' (i.e. having

enough cash always on hand to ensure that the project is able to be resourced in a manner sufficient for progression, dealing with the unexpected and delivering on time – we can all live in hope). On a more serious note, though, working capital has been a huge problem in my experience and – talking to people I know – still is.

2 Technology: Both an enabler and a driver – many projects exist alone for the purpose of technological R&D. As the business environment continues to evolve and is subject to constant volatility (much of it caused by technology), so competitive advantage is often defined by technological capability and capacity – faster, cheaper, to a sustained level of quality – all stem from technological leadership. Technology, though, is not without its drawbacks. If it is untested then the market may not adopt it. There may be a cost level involved in terms of replacing architecture and training staff that is simply too high. Coupled with this, there is always going to be uncertainty as to the length of period that a particular technology is the cutting edge – an organisation that invests heavily in the above mentioned might suddenly find that competitors have a newer, better process/hardware/methodology that might even have been cheaper. So, it's worth remembering that technology's sword cuts both ways. Traditionally, there was a school of strategic thought which believed that 'first mover advantage' was critical in order to gain a major or competitive market share. What this encapsulated was the ethos that you (the organisation) had to be the first to get your product onto the market before any competitor's, as this would then place your organisation in the driving seat in terms of competitive advantage. In today's markets – particularly when many products that appeal to the consumer are directly attributable to technological features and capabilities – the 'first mover' advantage is not seen as the panacea to corporate success that it once was. Sometimes a strategy used now is to let the competitor release its product – give it some time in the market – then, to utilise research as to what features/problems, etc. that the customer doesn't like/is unhappy with, ensure that your competing product has all of these issues sorted out, removed or improved upon. Some food for thought.

Regardless of the type of project and the level of resources required/used, the author would suggest that it is vital that resources are carefully managed. For one obvious reason – project budgets tend to be finite. Also, resource availability may not be abundant and effortless to acquire. Resource management is a key component to be matched to the operational requirements throughout the project lifecycle. Efficiency in resource allocation is therefore a key scheduling skill and should play a central role in both the planning and delivery process. In my opinion truly efficient resource management is reflected by a clear understanding of the purchasing rationale – how this is formulated and the actual procurement strategy and processes, coupled with attention being paid to inventory and its management and any applicable lead time implications.

Silver bullet: Resource management should be considered a key project function that comprises both strategic and tactical processes such as procurement strategy and inventory management.

Silver bullet: The starting point to promote efficiency in resource management is the active search and elimination of any duplication taking place across project activities and sub-activities.

Earlier, we looked at the WBS and discussed its advantages and why it was very useful from a project delivery perspective. Allow me to share an old trick with you – the WBS can be significantly enhanced by the inclusion of an RBS (resource breakdown structure) superimposed over it. This is something that the author always did as standard practice when taking on a project. So, what do I mean? It's not quite as fancy as it sounds but it is a good common-sense approach to establishing and maintaining control as the project moves through its lifecycle. In Figure 8.2, I have designated a work package and shown the RBS included.

Although basic in the extreme, what the reader will see as the fundamental difference between this and the stock standard WBS (shown earlier) is the amount of additional usefulness in adding the RBS. Just like the WBS, the RBS can be 'exploded' down to as many or as few levels as you – the PM – decides. So, looking at

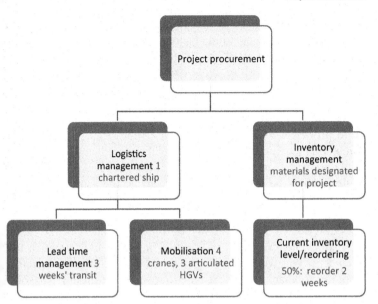

Figure 8.2 A simple illustration of a WBS/RBS

Figure 8.2, if we know we need a ship and we need it for three weeks and we know what equipment we will require to unload the cargo when it arrives, it becomes relatively easy to determine what the costs are going to be by making the calculation based on the cost of identified resource requirements and time periods. You could almost consider this as a type of 'resource profiling' methodology.

Silver bullet: An RBS complements the project WBS and provides significantly more information at a glance. It is a useful complement for effective project management, monitoring and controlling as well as aiding clarity in planning and pre-scheduling activities and budgetary management.

Project crashing

I thought that a brief overview of this technique would round off the discussion about resource management nicely. So, just exactly what do I mean by 'project crashing'? The essence of this technique is about the assignment of extra resources at a premium cost to accelerate project completion. There are generally two reasons why you might want to 'crash' a project. First, the project is behind schedule and you wish to avoid damage to reputation or punitive measures such as the activation of LDCs (liquidated damage clauses) (a more common reason), or second, there is some form of incentive/bonus scheme stipulated within the contract and it would be more profitable to finish early. A third motivation might be that completing a particular project early will free tied-up resources that can be moved to another project (i.e. manpower and plant). Project crashing might be achieved by things such as the approval of overtime hours or the hiring of additional resources (such as plant and labour).

A cautionary note: even when deciding to crash a project due to the reasons mentioned above, careful consideration is essential. For instance, if you were facing a penalty of some financial amount it would be foolhardy in the extreme to spend more money on avoiding the penalty than the penalty amount itself. However, there may be some cases where just this situation may arise – possibly within the context of organisational reputation or ensuring the continuance of a positive long-term relationship with a key client. You may make the decision to soak up the additional cost and offset it against what you may stand to lose in the longer run if you don't. Business and project management is, after all, fundamentally about managing relationships.

Project fast tracking

This is another 'schedule compression technique' that is commonly used. It is easy to do but can alter the risk profile of a project (because you don't know for sure what's going to happen within the project's immediate environment). Simply put, project fast tracking (PFT) is taking a look at the schedule and reordering some of the activities. The reader may recall that an earlier silver bullet expressed the fact that there were only two types of project activities: sequential ones and parallel ones. Project fast tracking seeks to reorganise sequential activities into parallel ones where possible within the project schedule. This can be tremendously effective, as it neither impacts upon the project schedule nor the project scope. There are two key elements of PFT. First, you must identify those elements or activities that have the longest duration and are on the critical path of the schedule. Second, you will need to assess which of these activities are the easiest and least risky to shorten (always bear the project risk profile in mind when changing anything). The last consideration, having identified what can be changed and made a risk assessment, is to be savvy with the available schedule time. Activities that have been converted from sequential to parallel do not necessary all have to commence at once. It may be far more prudent to 'stage' them so that any potential disruption is minimised.

Lead time management

No discussion on resource management would be complete without examining this topic. Generally, resources are things that are non-static (i.e. they are fabricated/manufactured in one place and utilised – or stored prior to utilisation – in another place). The time that it takes for something to travel from 'point of origin' (i.e. factory) to 'point of destination' (i.e. a remote project inventory such as a 'lay-down' area in a pipeline or power transmission line project) is the definition of 'lead time.' Lead time is therefore about time and movement (speed/delay/mode of transport, etc.) and it is therefore always going to be quantified in terms of cost (consider, for instance, the differential between the various 'modes' of transportation – i.e. the premium cost that is always relative to air transportation). Lead time might also be reflected from an operational stance in terms of once the 'lead time' to an activity within the project schedule is complete – the Gantt Chart is a useful tool here.

The crux of the problem with lead time is one of control. As the author has stated previously, whenever a process becomes complex, by definition it becomes harder to control and therefore manage, and lead time is quite often (dependent of course on a huge range of case-specific factors) a complex activity, especially when it is international and 'multi-modal' (i.e. multiple types of transportation representing different 'stages' of the goods or item(s) journey from point of origin to point of destination), or is in a remote locale that lacks any sort of facilitating infrastructure. Thus it will become apparent to the reader that the focused management of lead time is an important aspect of project scheduling and control in order to ensure uninterrupted operational activity as the project moves through its lifecycle towards delivery.

If we consider this discussion so far, the author would suggest that we 'look behind' the factors that have been mentioned. A disconnect I am never happy with (and seems to be regrettably ubiquitous) is that between the contract and the project. The author would suggest that it is imperative for those engaged in pre-project activity to carefully identify lead time requirements and make an assessment of the likelihood of possible risks associated with non-performance (non-delivery) or partial performance (late delivery) in terms of contractual liability, impact on physical project delivery and impact on stakeholders (such as the client). Although a supplier will state a TOD (time of delivery), the reader must remember that any lead time is going to be subject to variation – there is such a huge range of potential factors that could either directly or indirectly impact upon an items' journey that sensible contingency planning will ensure a project doesn't get caught out by some unwelcome news or event. Insurance, guarantees and warranties granted obviously go some way towards ameliorating such issues – but this needs to be very carefully thought out and a strategy put in place that will be reflected in any commercial negotiations prior to project initiation.

Silver bullet: Some lead times are 'critical.' A critical lead time is central to the project's operational abilities in terms of delivery. It should be considered as a critical success factor.

Managing project inventories

There are several key issues that have to be dealt with when considering the management of project inventories. Foremost among these tends to be location. As mentioned above in our discussion about lead time, often a project inventory could be located somewhere significantly remote – away from the main warehousing/storage facilities of the parent organisation and within a locale that is difficult to reach, perhaps due to little or no supporting infrastructure. This problem becomes compounded if any of the materials in question require specialised storage such as climate control (i.e. frozen/chilled/maintained at a specific temperature/heated, etc.) or are dangerous – either inherently (explosives) or are an environmental risk. The choice facing the organisation is basically twofold: build compliant storage facilities on location or have 'mobile' (i.e. trucks/trains) storage facilities. Neither of these may be ultimately desirable and there will be a significant cost factor, but unfortunately, in the author's experience, there is little other choice.

The issue of 'temporary' (i.e. staging area/lay-down area) vs. 'permanent' (i.e. supply base) is a knotty conundrum to unravel. Another underlying factor that can be significant is the issue of security. The author is very familiar with remote projects having their inventory stolen or vandalised to such an extent as to delay project delivery and throw the budget out of the window. I mention this because security in itself (or the need for it) can be a determining factor as to the degree of investment the organisation is willing to make. I would suggest that the following factors represent some if not most of the key decision-making aspects of this problem.

Decision criteria for establishing project inventories

1. Remoteness – where does the inventory need to be located (at what proximity to project operations)?
2. Are there any pre-existing storage facilities available?
3. Do these pre-existing storage facilities have any specialist capabilities (i.e. temperature control)?
4. Do these pre-existing storage facilities offer protection to the inventory (i.e. from the elements, from theft/damage, etc.)?
5. Is there a compromise in terms of a location that is closer that could be utilised?
6. Is security an issue?
7. If the area in question is very remote and isolated, what medical facilities are available?
8. If the area in question is very remote and isolated, what psychological assessment has been made of personnel to judge their suitability for working within this environment?
9. What degree of IT/communications infrastructure will be required?
10. Have all relevant stakeholders been identified and is a stakeholder management plan ready to be implemented?
11. Are there any significant environmental issues associated with project activities within the area?

12   What is the size and duration of the project in question (i.e. is it a capital project)?

13   Does the organisation wish to establish a permanent presence in the area (i.e. will there be future projects in the area)?

14   Could the location of permanent facilities in the area be a source of competitive advantage?

The author hopes that you, the reader, have enjoyed reading this book and that you will derive some quantum of value from the experiences, suggested strategies and ideas contained within. The next book in the 'Silver Bullets' series is currently a work in progress and should be out there in due course. I wish you well in your endeavours – best of luck with your projects!

INDEX